BUGSY AND THE LITTLE MAN

A screenplay

By
Benjamin Kerstein

CREDITS play WHITE OVER BLACK, interspersed with old photographs from the 1920s: the golden age of the gangster. A lone piano quietly picks out the melody of "Bye Bye Blackbird."

FADE IN

EXT. JERUSALEM STREET - DAY

A tire screeches past us, followed by a fusillade of car horns.

We TILT UP and see several Hasidic Jews, clad in traditional clothing, walking towards us. As they pass by, a short, stocky, balding man of around 65, wearing large sunglasses, crosses their path. We FOLLOW HIM as he crosses the street in quick, short steps.

A TITLE READS: "JERUSALEM, 1970."

The stocky man steps on to the opposite sidewalk. He takes a small slip of paper out of his pocket and examines it. He looks around, squinting behind his oversize sunglasses.

CUT TO

INT. NEWSPAPER OFFICE - DAY

We TRACK SLOWLY between the desks of a bustling, cacophonous newsroom. People are rushing this way and that. Typewriters clack like machine guns. We STOP at the desk of a very young, somewhat disheveled looking reporter. He is leaning back in his chair talking excitedly in Hebrew into the telephone. His name is YOSSI KLEIN.

We PULL BACK to reveal a SECRETARY waiting patiently for him. He puts his hand over the receiver for a moment...

(The following dialogue takes place in subtitled Hebrew.)

KLEIN
        What is it?

SECRETARY
        There's someone here to see you.

KLEIN
        There's someone here to see me? Kissinger lands in six hours. Tell him to fuck off.

He goes back to the phone.

SECRETARY
        He says his name is Meyer Lansky.

KLEIN stops dead in his conversation. He looks up at the SECRETARY with a shocked expression on his face.

CUT TO

INT. WAITING ROOM - DAY

We FOLLOW KLEIN as he walks out of the newsroom into the waiting room. We STOP just over his shoulder, revealing the short, stocky man we have just seen seated uncomfortably in a chair, his hands clasped together in front of him. As we now know, his name is MEYER LANSKY.

YOSSI
        Ehh... excuse me... are you... Mr. Lansky?

LANSKY looks up. When he answers, his voice is rough, hewn out by years of cigarette smoking.

MEYER
        Are you Yussi Klein?

KLEIN
        Yossi Klein. Yes.

LANSKY slowly, painfully gets to his feet. His body is stiff, but we sense that he has strength behind his aged movements.

MEYER
        I was hoping you might have some time.

KLEIN
        Time?

MEYER
        To listen to my story.

FADE TO

EXT. CAFE BALCONY - DAY

KLEIN and MEYER are led to a table by a pretty young WAITRESS. They sit opposite each other at the balcony's edge. MEYER gazes at the magnificent view of the Old City and, beyond it, East Jerusalem and the Mount of Olives.

MEYER
        It's beautiful.

KLEIN
        Yes. It is, isn't it?

He sweeps his arm across the vista.

KLEIN
        Before the war, all of this was Jordan. There used to be snipers on those walls, and
        barbed wire all the way down that street...

MEYER nods. But he seems far away. Lost in thought. KLEIN lights a cigarette.

MEYER

You got another one of those?

KLEIN nods and hands one to him.

MEYER

I got a doctor back in the States who's trying to get me off these things. He says: "They'll take ten years off your life!" I told him: "Doc, I'm 65 years old. What's the fuckin' difference?"

They both laugh. Then there is an awkward pause. MEYER looks directly at KLEIN.

MEYER

You know who I am, don't you?

KLEIN

I know your name. Your reputation.

MEYER

My reputation... A man never escapes his reputation.

KLEIN

I know you are under indictment in the United States for tax fraud and racketeering, amongst other things...

MEYER

Amongst other things?

KLEIN

Amongst many other things. I know you've been trying to claim Israeli citizenship under the Law of Return for the past six months, and that approval... has not been forthcoming.

MEYER

"Has not been forthcoming." That's a very nice way of putting it, Mr. Klein.

YOSSI

Yossi. Please.

MEYER

That's a nice way of putting it, Yussi.

He sighs.

MEYER

My whole life I've snuck in the back door. This time, I want to come in the front door. Clean, legitimate, justified... But your prime minister does not want a man of my...reputation living in this country.

Pause.

KLEIN

Is that why you want to tell your story?

Another pause.

MEYER

Yes.

KLEIN

    Well...?

MEYER

    I don't know where to begin.

KLEIN

    Begin at the beginning.

MEYER

    The beginning... the beginning was just like the end. And now, it's after the end. You should know, I'm an old man, so it's hard for me, sometimes, to remember. But I think... I think this is how it happened...

                                                    CUT TO

EXT. NEW YORK STREET - DAY

A fist lands on the jaw of a thirteen year old boy. His newsboy hat flies off and he stumbles backwards, blood streaming from his nose and mouth. Two boys grab his arms and hold him up.

The boy is MEYER as a young man. He is surrounded by young Italian toughs. One of them is beating him savagely.

A TITLE READS: "THE LOWER EAST SIDE - BROOKLYN, NEW YORK 1916"

The older boy punches him again in the stomach, MEYER crumples onto the ground.

ITALIAN BOY

    The Jews don't cross into fuckin' Mott Street! Not today, not tomorrow, not ever!

He kicks him.

ITALIAN BOY #2

    Stay outta our territory ya sheeny!

MEYER rolls on to his stomach and slowly, painfully gets to his feet. He looks the ITALIAN BOY in the eye as he wipes the blood from his nose.

ITALIAN BOY

    What you got to say?

MEYER looks at him for a long moment. Then, in a sudden burst of movement, HE PUNCHES HIM IN THE FACE, breaking his nose.

The ITALIAN BOY screams and stumbles backward. MEYER bores in on him, punching him in the stomach. The Italian boys try to tear them apart, but MEYER won't let go. Finally, five of the boys pull him away and force him to the ground under a rain of blows. MEYER's fists are still flailing as he tries to force them off.

BOYS

    Hold him godammit! Keep him down!

Out of the crowd, a tall, lanky youngster with a left eye permanently half-shut pushes his way through the watching toughs. His name is SALVATORE LUCIANO, and we will know him as LUCKY.

LUCKY
That's it! That's enough! Let him up!

The BOYS obey instantly and release MEYER. They huddle behind LUCKY.

MEYER gets to his feet, his nose and mouth bleeding profusely, his eyes burning with anger and defiance. LUCKY approaches him slowly, looking him over.

LUCKY
Tough little sheeny, aint ya?

MEYER doesn't answer. He just glowers at the slit-eyed kid in front of him.

LUCKY
What's your name kid?

MEYER
None of your fuckin' business!

LUCKY smiles. He chuckles softly. He lightly taps him on the cheek.

LUCKY
Get out of here kid. Tell your friends, if they want to run their game on Mott Street they talk to Lucky first. Got it?

MEYER does not answer, but looks daggers back at him.

LUCKY
Go on. Go.

LUCKY steps back. His gang follows him. They look confused.

LUCKY
Let him go, boys!

MEYER watches as the phalanx of toughs separates to allow him through. He turns slowly and starts to limp away from the crowd. We PULL BACK with him as he walks away. LUCKY watches him go, his hands in his pockets.

                                                                    FADE TO

INT. TENEMENT APARTMENT - DUSK

A middle aged woman, her head wrapped in a shawl, is intoning the Sabbath prayer in a low whisper, her eyes tight shut. She is MEYER's mother SARAH.

CLOSE UP of her hands. They waver over a pair of candles. In the background we hear a door being opened. She finishes the prayer and looks up.

MEYER is framed in the doorway, his face a mass of bruises and cuts.

SARAH
     Meyer! My God!

She rushes over to him and cradles his face in her hands.

SARAH
     My treasure, what did they do to you?

MEYER
     I was in a fight.

SARAH
     With who?

MEYER
     The Mott Street Boys.

SARAH
     Animals, animals...

She runs some water over a cloth and begins dabbing his wounds with it.

Behind her, a door opens. A bearded man in a skullcap and black clothes, clearly a pious man, stands framed in the doorway. It is MEYER's father, JOSEPH. MEYER looks up and sees him.

CLOSE UP of JOSEPH. He looks MEYER up and down. His face is like stone.

MEYER blinks, shaking slightly. A trickle of blood rolls down his forehead across the bridge of his nose. SARAH, clutching the bloody rag, says nothing. JOSEPH turns and disappears, shutting the door behind him.

MEYER's eyes brim with tears. He wipes them away with his sleeve and dashes out of the apartment.

SARAH
     Meyer!

Her son is gone. She puts her hand to her forehead and wearily leans on the kitchen table.

                                                                    CUT TO

EXT. DELANCY STREET - NIGHT

MEYER is running, tears streaming down his face. He finally collapses into a dark corner between two buildings and starts weeping like a child, covering his face with his hands.

We PULL BACK and we see the streets filled with religious Jews, clad in their best Sabbath clothes, walking home from synagogue. Candles are being lit in the windows. Families are sitting for dinner.

We RISE UP into an enormous CRANE SHOT of the Lower East Side on a Sabbath evening: men in their prayer shawls, girls running home with the groceries, peddlers hawking their last wares, women hustling their children home. A panorama of a lost world.

CUT TO

EXT. THE STREET - DAY

CLOSE UP of MEYER's eyes. His bruises are turning green as they heal. He is staring intently at something. We hear voices yelling in the background.

A group of boys are playing craps. The dealer, JOEY LEVINE, barely a year older than MEYER, is rubbing the dice between his hands.

LEVINE
> All bets in, all bets in!

People are handing money to each other and to LEVINE's partner, a portly boy named LENNY AARONSOHN. MEYER does not remove his hands from his pockets. He watches the proceedings intensely. We can almost see the wheels turning in his mind.

LEVINE
> Final roll, final roll! All bets in!

A tall, lanky boy, dark-eyed and swarthy, not a day over fifteen, clad in a long coat and carrying an air of brash confidence, pushes his way to the front of the crowd. His name will one day be famous.

He is BENJAMIN "BUGSY" SIEGEL.

BUGSY
> What's your limit, Levine?

LEVINE looks up at the cocky youngster in front of him.

LEVINE
> More than you got.

The crowd laughs. BUGSY smiles. He is not even slightly intimidated. He pulls a wad of bills out of his pocket.

BUGSY
> That's a shame, 'cos I'm lookin' for a shnorrer just like you to lay a few dimes on.

There is a murmur of shock from the crowd. BUGSY peels a bill off his roll and holds it out, neatly folded in his hand.

BUGSY
> Fifty. Gen-u-ine U.S. greenbacks.

LEVINE
> You rip that off your grandmother, Benny?

BUGSY
> Aint none of your concern, Levine.

LEVINE looks at the bill outstretched before him for a long minute. Then he snaps it out of BUGSY's hand.

LEVINE

You're on, Benny. One roll only, winner-takes-all.

BUGSY

Good. I feel lucky.

LEVINE smiles out of the corner of his mouth, just for a second. He rubs the dice between his hands.

LEVINE

Alright, alright! All bets in, all bets in!

MEYER's eyes are fixed on the dice.

LEVINE bends his knees slightly and hurls the dice against a tenement wall. The crowd pushes in. MEYER cranes his neck to see.

LENNY

Snake eyes! Snake eyes! Dealer takes all!

There is a disappointed moan from the crowd. They begin to disperse. LEVINE emerges from the crowd with BUGSY's fifty dollar bill. He holds it up triumphantly in front of his adversary's face.

LEVINE

Sorry, Benny. Some fellas just aint lucky.

BUGSY stares at him with eyes like ice.

LEVINE

Well...I guess there's more where that came from.

BUGSY turns to leave, his teeth clenched in anger.

MEYER is standing right in front of him, blocking the way.

MEYER

He burned you.

LEVINE

What?

BUGSY

What?

MEYER

I been watchin' him for three days. He aint never hit snake eyes more than three times in a day. Today he hit it seven times and it aint even five o'clock. No honest craps game on this street ever hits more than five in a day.

LEVINE

Who the fuck is this punk?

BUGSY

    Shut your filthy mouth Levine. (To MEYER:) What are you sayin'?

MEYER

    I'm sayin' them dice are holdin' water. No doubt about it.

LEVINE

    What'd you say?

BUGSY

    You playin' loaded, Levine?

LEVINE

    Fuck you, Siegel!

BUGSY

    Let's see them dice, Levine. Now.

LEVINE

    I don't gotta show you nothin', Siegel. (To MEYER:) And you, you little mamzer, you best stay off the streets from now on!

BUGSY

    You're talkin' to me now, Levine.

MEYER

    Fuck you, Levine! Aint nothin' more crooked than a crooked craps gun!

LEVINE

    You lookin' to get fixed, you little shit?

He reaches into his pocket and pulls out a small revolver. A woman screams and the crowd begins to scatter. MEYER, shocked, stumbles backward.

BUGSY PUNCHES LEVINE IN THE STOMACH, doubling him over. LEVINE gasps. BUGSY grabs him by the collar and slams him up against the tenement wall and punches him again. LEVINE slides on to the pavement, the wind knocked out of him. Far off, we hear a police whistle. LEVINE explodes into a coughing fit. BUGSY rifles the pockets of LEVINE's jacket and finds his fifty. He stuffs it in his pocket and turns to MEYER.

BUGSY

    Run, goddam it! Didn't your momma teach you nothin'?

MEYER just stands there, wide-eyed. BUGSY grabs him by the shoulder and they take off down the street.

LEVINE slowly clambers to his feet and aims his revolver.

MEYER and BUGSY duck as LEVINE fires wildly. We hear the bullets ricochet off the tenement walls. BUGSY throws MEYER into an alley.

                              CUT TO

INT. ALLEY - DAY

BUGSY pulls MEYER down the alley and, looking behind him, takes a quick turn into an alcove. He pushes MEYER back and peers out around the corner.

BUGSY
> Stay there, alright? Don't move.

He peers around the corner. MEYER sees the handle of a pistol sticking out of his belt.

BUGSY
> I think we lost him.

MEYER is deathly pale. BUGSY straightens MEYER's collar.

BUGSY
> Never been shot at before, huh?

MEYER shakes his head.

BUGSY
> Well, there's a first time for everything, aint there? Aint nobody ever had the guts to burn me at craps before.

He smiles. MEYER laughs.

BUGSY
> What's your name?

MEYER
> Meyer Lansky.

BUGSY
> Alright, Meyer Lansky. I'm Benny Siegel.

MEYER nods.

MEYER
> I know who you are.

BUGSY
> Nah, you know my rep. C'mon, he's gone.

They walk out into the alley side by side. BUGSY towers over MEYER's slight frame.

BUGSY
> You connected?

MEYER
> What?

BUGSY
> Connected. You work for somebody?

MEYER
> I deliver groceries for Goldberg's on Thursdays.

BUGSY laughs.

BUGSY

> That aint what I meant. Who taught you to size up the dealers?

MEYER

> I just watch the games.

BUGSY

> How much watchin' it take you to figure Levine?

MEYER

> Bout two days. He always hits high. Nobody hits high forever less he's playin' loaded.

BUGSY shakes his head in fascinated amazement.

BUGSY

> Two days. That's somethin' aint it?

> > > > CUT TO

EXT. THE STREET - DAY

MEYER and BUGSY are standing at the entrance to an alley, looking across the street at a DEALER throwing craps.

MEYER

> See, every fifth or sixth throw hits for the crowd, the rest are all on the dealer's end, but not big wins. That's just numbers.

BUGSY

> The odds.

MEYER

> Right, see sooner or later, the crowd is bound to win, but the numbers are all on the dealer's side.

BUGSY

> He's rigged up.

MEYER

> No, he aint rigged, he's just got the numbers tilted his way. It aint dirty. But in the end he always comes out on top. Only the suckers think they can get lucky. The dealer, he knows there aint no such thing as luck. Only numbers.

BUGSY

> And the numbers are on his side.

MEYER points to another DEALER further down the street.

MEYER

> Right. Now this guy, he only hits once in every ten, fifteen throws. But they're big wins, cleans out the crowd. He's smart though. He's spacin' it out. Waits till one bunch gets tired and another comes in, so they can't put the numbers together.

BUGSY
        I don't get it.

MEYER
        See, aint no way a man hits that big, over and over again. He takes the stake once every
        ten or twelve rolls. Never fails. He's got more than the numbers workin' for him.

BUGSY
        That so?

BUGSY's eyes become icy again. The crowd groans as the DEALER cleans them out.

BUGSY
        Come on kid. Now I'm gonna show you what I'm good at.

He starts across the street. MEYER anxiously tags behind.

We CLOSE IN on the DEALER counting his winnings as the crowd dissipates. He looks up and
sees BUGSY approaching. A look of exasperation crosses his face.

DEALER
        Alright, Siegel, waddya want? I paid Stecchio on Thursday. What the fuck?

BUGSY grabs him by the collar and pulls him into a nearby alley.

BUGSY
        How ya doin' Larry? Let's talk for a minute.

                                                                    CONTINUE INTO

INT. ALLEY - DAY

BUGSY throws the DEALER against the wall and rifles in his pockets.

DEALER
        What's the big deal, Siegel?

BUGSY find the DEALER's dice in his pockets. He grabs the wad of bills out of the DEALER's
hand.

DEALER
        Hey! Them greenbacks is mine! I paid the Moustache Pete already!

BUGSY starts slowly rifling through the wad of bills, smiling to himself.

BUGSY
        Doin' pretty good, aint ya Larry?

DEALER
        Yeah. I got a good corner.

BUGSY
        A good corner? Larry, this is more than just a good corner.

DEALER

What? The luck's with me today.

BUGSY

Luck? My friend here says there aint no such thing as luck. Just numbers.

MEYER stands at the alley's entrance, silently looking on.

DEALER

I dunno. I gotta good corner... That's all.

BUGSY

Yeah. A good corner.

He looks at the dice in his hand.

BUGSY

These dice of yours, Larry. Been good to you?

DEALER

Sure. Sure, they done me good.

BUGSY

They feel a little heavy, Larry.

DEALER

Now look, Benny...

BUGSY

You been givin' yourself a little extra luck on the side, Larry?

DEALER

Bugsy, please...

BUGSY throws the dice in the DEALER's face, then hurls the money after it. The DEALER grabs at the bills, losing his balance. BUGSY pulls a small switchblade from his coat pocket and, holding it to the DEALER's throat, pins him against the wall.

BUGSY

My name is not Bugsy, you understand?! A bug is not a name, you stupid fat prick! A bug is an insect! Something that crawls in the dirt and the shit! Is that what you think I am?!

DEALER

No! No!

BUGSY

You dumb sonofabitch!

He slashes him across the face in two sudden strokes. MEYER jumps with shock. The DEALER falls to his knees, holding his bleeding cheeks in his hands.

BUGSY bends down and picks up the bills from the ground. He folds them neatly and puts them in his pocket. He is breathing hard and shallow, his eyes bulging, his nostrils flared with rage.

BUGSY

From now on, you play a dirty game, you pay like you're playin' a dirty game.

The DEALER sobs behind his bloody hands.

BUGSY

Fucking shmuck.

He walks out of the alley past MEYER, who is transfixed with shock and horror.

BUGSY

You comin' or not?

MEYER takes a last look at the crumpled figure in the alley. Then he turns and follows after his new friend.

SLOW FADE TO

INT. TAVERN - NIGHT

BUGSY and MEYER enter into a dark, sleazy barroom. The signs in the windows are in Yiddish and a slow jazz tune plays on a Victrola in the background. MEYER follows BUGSY to the back, where a group of boys are sitting, playing cards.

BUGSY

What's the score, boys?

The BOYS laugh and raise their glasses.

BOY

Who's the stranger?

BUGSY

A find, that's what he is. A gift. Boys, this is Meyer Lansky. Meyer, this is Moesy Sedway, Lepke Bouchalter, and Artie Schultz. We call him Dutch.

MEYER

Why?

LEPKE

'Cos he's always in dutch.

They laugh. BUGSY sits down and pulls up a chair for MEYER.

BUGSY

We are prosperous today, boys. Thanks to our new friend. He pulls the wad of bills from his pocket.

DUTCH

Holy shit, Benjamin. Where'd you steal that?

BUGSY

Took it off a craps dealer on 45th. He was runnin' a dirty game and payin' honest wages to Stecchio.

MOESY

No shit. How'd ya make him?

BUGSY

Meyer here's got an eye for when the numbers don't add up.

MOESY

Not bad, little man. Not bad.

MEYER

Just got to add 'em up right...

MOESY

Hell, if I'd a known addin' sums would be so prosperous, I'd a stayed in PS 67.

He laughs uproariously. The others join him. MEYER blushes. BUGSY starts handing out bills as if dealing a deck of cards.

BUGSY

Enjoy it gentlemen. What Stecchio don't know aint gonna hurt him.

MEYER

Who's Stecchio?

DUTCH

Benny, where'd you find this green motherfucker? (to MEYER:) Stecchio, little man, is the wop what owns this town.

BUGSY

The first thing you got to understand, Meyer, is that all the money in this neighborhood is Italian money. It don't matter if its Jews throwin' the dice and Jews losin' their shirts. In the end, every dollar you throw at the dice is a wop dollar. Nothin' thinks, talks, walks or shits without them knowin' and without them gettin' a cut. That's how it is. The wops got the Jews by the balls in this city, and you got to work for them if you want to work.

MEYER

I don't get it. Why throw down for someone else?

BUGSY smiles out of the corner of his mouth.

BUGSY

Why? Cos if we don't, Stecchio'll do to me what I did to that craps flinger today. 'Cept he won't be gentle like I was.

DUTCH

In this town, everybody pays, but everybody makes money.

MOESY

Just that the wops, they make a little more money.

BUGSY

Goddam guinea bastards.

They all crack up laughing.

BUGSY

Let's drink to the greasy motherfuckers! Someone get a bottle!

A bottle of whiskey is produced. BUGSY starts to pour out.

BUGSY

    (To MEYER) Do yourself a favor little man, don't take it all at once.

MEYER looks at the other boys knocking back their drinks. He pauses for a moment and then does the same. He finishes the glass and explodes into a coughing fit. The boys all laugh. BUGSY pats MEYER on the back.

BUGSY

    It's alright, he aint used to it.

MEYER wipes the side of his mouth.

BUGSY

    Second one's easier, don't worry...

He starts to pour MEYER another glass.

                        FADE TO

LATER

The boys are now very drunk, but they are listening, transfixed, to MEYER.

MEYER

    See, its all in the numbers. No matter what, the house comes out on top. Okay, you could get lucky in your first or second throw and win big. But you got to cut and run right then, or sooner or later it all goes back to the house. See, they know that if a guy comes to throw down, he can't stop with one big score. He always thinks there's gonna be another one. And there aint gonna be another one. 'Less the game is dirty.

LEPKE

    Yeah, but if you play for, you know, years, you're gonna win big someday...

MEYER

    Na, that's the beauty of it. The more you play the more you lose, 'cos the numbers favor the house. The longer you keep at it, the more you hand over.

BUGSY

    It's a sucker's game, boys. The key is to be the house and not the sucker.

MEYER

    It's the best racket the devil ever made. Why knock over a bank? They'll just come and hand the money over, so long as they think there's a big score behind it. But there aint. There's never a big score waiting. Just a hole to throw your change into.

BUGSY

    We been wastin' our time boys. The money aint in shakin' down the craps flingers. It's in runnin' the games.

DUTCH

    What you thinkin', Benny?

BUGSY
     I'm thinkin' it's high time we showed a little enterprise boys. (He lifts his glass.) To enterprise! L'chaim!!!

EVERYONE
     L'chaim!!!

They all knock back their drinks.

BUGSY
     C'mon, let's take the little man to Judy's, show him a good time.

DUTCH shakes his head and puts his cigarette in his mouth.

DUTCH
     Benny, if you wasn't crazy, you'd still be pickin' shit in Delancy Street.

They all laugh and get up to leave.

                                 CUT TO

INT. JUDY'S WHOREHOUSE - NIGHT

The boys burst through the doors of a semi-upscale lower East Side whorehouse. A group of girls surround them, particularly BUGSY.

BUGSY pulls a tall brunette over to MEYER and puts his arm around MEYER's shoulders. He whispers in her ear and slips a wad of bills into her palm. He turns to MEYER. He is very drunk and slurs his words.

BUGSY
     Meyer, this is Deborah. She's a very good friend of mine.

MEYER seems to shrink by about a foot.

MEYER
     Hello.

DEBORAH smiles broadly.

                                   CUT TO

LATER

BUGSY and the crew sitting around a table with the girls. They are drinking and laughing, smoking cigars. MOESY blows smoke rings into the air. A dark haired girl is draped over BUGSY's shoulder.

DEBORAH is taking MEYER up the dark staircase by the hand. He looks back at the revelry and seems to pull back for a moment, but he follows her.

The girl leaning on BUGSY's shoulder is telling a joke in Yiddish. As she hits the punchline the table erupts in uproarious, drunken laughter. BUGSY grabs her and kisses her roughly on the cheek. Her name is LEAH.

CUT TO

INT. DEBORAH'S ROOM - NIGHT

The door opens and DEBORAH walks in, pulling MEYER by the hand. It is a small room, sparsely furnished. A round mirror hangs over the bed. There is a single chest of drawers in the corner. A flowing, white curtain hangs over the only window. A mezuza shines slightly in the door jamb.

DEBORAH leaves MEYER standing by the bed and goes over to the chest of drawers. She takes out her earrings and places them carefully in a small wooden box.

DEBORAH
    Take off your clothes.

CUT TO

INT. DOWNSTAIRS - NIGHT

The boys are having a time. MOESY is kissing his girl, his hand up her blouse. BUGSY blows a massive cloud of cigarette smoke into the air.

CUT TO

INT. DEBORAH'S ROOM - NIGHT

MEYER doesn't move. DEBORAH turns and looks at him, her hands fiddling in her hair.

DEBORAH
    Don't be scared.

MEYER looks at the floor. DEBORAH undoes her hair. It falls in a cascade of curls around her face. Her eyes are luminous.

DEBORAH
    You know how, don't you?

MEYER looks up again. He nods. DEBORAH smiles, half exasperated and half sweet.

CUT TO

INT. DOWNSTAIRS - NIGHT

LEAH is seated on the bar, her eyes closed, singing an old Yiddish song. It is a keening ballad, filled with loss and regret.

CLOSE UP of THE BOYS. They are watching LEAH. Completely silent.

A long TRACKING SHOT files one by one past their faces. They look wistful and lost.

CUT TO

INT. DEBORAH'S ROOM - NIGHT

DEBORAH pulls her dress up over her head and lays it carefully on a rocking chair in the corner. MEYER begins unbuttoning his shirt and pulling off his shoes.

DEBORAH pulls her underwear off and, shivering in the cold, gets into bed. MEYER, now naked, gets in next to her. He looks petrified. DEBORAH runs her hand through his hair and kisses him lightly on the lips.

DEBORAH
        You can touch mine first if you want.

She guides his hand down between her legs. She puts her cheek next to his. Her breathing becomes hard and shallow. He begins to relax.

LONG SHOT of the two of them face to face on the bed, the covers pulled up to their chins. A slight breeze almost imperceptibly lifts the threadbare white curtain.

                                                                                CUT TO

INT. DOWNSTAIRS - NIGHT

CLOSE UP of LEAH as she sings.

                                                                                CUT TO

INT. DEBORAH'S ROOM - NIGHT

MEYER awkwardly climbs on top of DEBORAH. She reaches down and maneuvers him inside her. He begins to thrust uncertainly.

DEBORAH
        That's it, honey. Take your time.

She whispers reassuringly in his ear as he continues. Her eyes close. She starts to moan quietly.

                                                                                CUT TO

INT. DOWNSTAIRS - NIGHT

LEAH finishes the song, hanging on a final, aching note before the end.

The boys are silent, moved. BUGSY stubs his cigar out. Swaying drunkenly, he stands up, pulling back the edge of his jacket to reveal the butt of a revolver.

BUGSY
        What the fuck is this? This a night for celebration!

He pulls the revolver out and waves it above his head. LEAH laughs hysterically.

BUGSY FIRES INTO THE AIR. Dust cascades down from the ceiling. LEAH squeals and keeps laughing.

The boys jump up and wrestle him down, pulling the gun out of his hand. BUGSY continues to bellow like an animal. The girls are all beside themselves with laughter.

CUT TO

INT. DEBORAH'S ROOM - NIGHT

MEYER moans, his head bowed, as he finishes. He crumples up next to DEBORAH. She strokes the back of his head. Her eyes are serene.

CUT TO

LATER

DEBORAH is asleep. MEYER rises and pulls on his pants. Quietly, he opens the door and goes out.

CUT TO

INT. HALLWAY - NIGHT

MEYER stumbles in the dark, looking for the bathroom. He tries a door and it's locked. He tries another and it opens. He goes inside. A moment later he comes out, buttoning his pants. He looks up and stops.

MEYER'S POV of BUGSY is seated in a rocking chair in the hallway, next to a closed door. His face looks satisfied and peaceful.

BUGSY
How are you, little man?

His face is half shrouded in shadow. Rocking back and forth, he looks more like an old man then a teenage hood.

MEYER
Ok.

BUGSY nods and smiles. He closes his eyes, continuing to rock.

MEYER
What you doin' out here, Benny?

BUGSY
I'm waitin' for the lady of the house. She's got Moesy in there.

MEYER nods.

BUGSY
My old man used to come to places like this. He'd always tip the whores ten cents, no matter what. They called him Mr. Ten Cents. He works seven days a week in the

garment district; my mama too. Seven days a week at five cents an hour for two rooms on the fifth floor, some cold meat, a dollar a week for my grandfather, ten cents a week for the whores...

He smiles.

BUGSY

It's a racket, Meyer. A fixed game. They got a con goin' and they got it locked up tight. But you and me... You and me is smart enough to know it's a racket. You and me is smart enough to say: it aint the game, it's the dealer. It aint the dice, it's the numbers. House always wins. The trick is to make sure you're the house.

Pause.

BUGSY

Always.

Pause. BUGSY leans back again.

BUGSY

I got to thinkin' about what you said... And you know what I think?

MEYER says nothing. BUGSY's head lolls to one side. He shuts his eyes again.

BUGSY

I think the whole thing is a racket. Not just the crap games and the whorehouses and the wops... It's all of this...

He opens his eyes into slits.

BUGSY

Everything.

MEYER steps forward slightly. Out of the shadows. His face is illuminated by a yellow lamp on the wall.

BUGSY

Crooked. Rigged. House always wins. You know what I think, little man?

MEYER shakes his head.

BUGSY

I think one day we're gonna be the house. And a million suckers gonna come crawling to us. Just to throw their change down the hole.

He closes his eyes and starts to rock again. MEYER waits for him to say something else, but BUGSY is silent. MEYER goes back into DEBORAH's room.

CUT TO

INT. DEBORAH'S ROOM - DAWN

MEYER is sleeping next to DEBORAH. The purple light of dawn is beginning to shine through the threadbare curtain. The door opens and BUGSY comes in, his shirt untucked and his hat perched comically on his head. He shakes MEYER awake.

BUGSY
        Wake up little man. We got work to do.

CUT TO

EXT. THE STREETS - DAY

The boys cross the street and surround a CRAPS DEALER. They are a mob now, moving almost in unison.

CRAPS DEALER
        What you boys want? I paid Maranzano already.

BUGSY
        Maybe you aint heard. Maranzano aint the only game in town no more.

CRAPS DEALER
        What?

BUGSY
        From now on, we get a dollar a week from your take. Us. Not some goombah from uptown, you got it?

The DEALER laughs.

CRAPS DEALER
        Are you crazy? Who the fuck are you?

BUGSY smiles widely, then kicks the DEALER brutally in the shins. He shrieks and falls to the ground. The boys crowd in over him and begin beating him.

BUGSY
        Who the fuck are we?! You're gonna find out, motherfucker!

CUT TO

BUGSY is talking to the owner of a newspaper stand. We can't hear what they say, but the OWNER is getting angry and gesticulating wildly. Behind them, MEYER and MOESY slowly COME INTO FOCUS. They are pouring kerosene over the stacks of newspapers.

OWNER
        Now get the fuck outta here, you little mamzer!

BUGSY
        I'll be back, shmuck.

He turns to walk away. MOESY throws a match on the papers and flees in the opposite direction. The OWNER turns and sees his store go up in a rush of orange flame.

CUT TO

INT. JEWELRY STORE - DAY

Customers are arguing furiously over the precious stones. The owner is gesticulating widely. Suddenly, three stones smash through the glass windows. The boys jump through the smashed windows. BUGSY comes in last, brandishing his revolver.

BUGSY
> Sorry, fellas. Business is closed for the day!

The boys start rifling through the jewels.

CUT TO

EXT. STREET - DAY

CLOSE UP of a CAR'S REARVIEW MIRROR. In it, we see BUGSY and MEYER approaching.

BUGSY looks around, then he smashes in the car window with a crowbar. He opens the door and gets in. He starts rifling the passenger glove compartment. He beckons to MEYER.

BUGSY
> Get in, goddamit!

MEYER gets in the driver's side and shuts the door.

CLOSE UP of the REARVIEW MIRROR. A POLICEMAN is framed in the glass.

MEYER sees him and freezes. The POLICEMAN blows his whistle.

BUGSY
> Shit! Let's get out of here! Start her up!

MEYER
> Benny, I can't drive!

BUGSY
> What?!

The POLICEMAN blows his whistle again.

BUGSY
> Goddam it!

He reaches over and grabs the wheel. MEYER wriggles out underneath him to the passenger seat. BUGSY slams the starter and they take off just in time.

CUT TO

INT. LANSKY APARTMENT - NIGHT

MEYER comes in quietly, shutting the door behind him. He turns and stops. SARAH sits at the table. Her knitting is in her lap.

SARAH
> Your father went to bed hours ago.

Pause.

SARAH
>
> Where were you?

MEYER
>
> Working.

SARAH
>
> Working he says...

She looks down at her knitting. She shakes her head. MEYER sits across from her and takes a neatly folded wad of bills out of his pocket. He places them carefully in his mother's hand. She unfolds the bills and looks at them, shocked.

SARAH
>
> Meyer...

MEYER
>
> It's alright, Ma. Things are gonna be good from now on.

She looks at him. She doesn't know what to say.

MEYER
>
> Just keep it between us, alright? Buy yourself... Buy yourself one of those nice dresses down on Lafayette you always lookin' at. Or...

His mother is crying.

MEYER
>
> Ma... It's just money...

She smiles and kisses him on the cheek.

SARAH
>
> You're a good boy. (She wipes her eyes.) Go to bed.

MEYER nods. He kisses her on the forehead and leaves the room. SARAH folds the bills again and puts them down the front of her dress.

CUT TO

INT. SIEGEL APARTMENT - NIGHT

MEYER and BUGSY are straightening their ties in a hallway mirror. BUGSY is nonchalantly chewing a piece of gum. They look like a vaudeville act.

BUGSY
>
> C'mon, the girls'll be here in a minute.

They walk down a short, cramped corridor to the front door. BUGSY's mother, HANNA, is waiting for them in her apron.

HANNA

Don't you boys look nice...

BUGSY
>Thanks ma, don't wait up alright?

She kisses him adoringly on the cheek.

HANNA
>My little Benny...

BUGSY
>Alright, Ma, alright.

She coos at him in Yiddish and goes back into the kitchen. BUGSY wipes his cheek.

BUGSY
>Benny Siegel: dirtiest cutthroat sonofabitch to walk outta Delancy Street, but he was good to his mother.

MEYER smiles. BUGSY opens the front door. Just arriving are two young neighborhood girls. They are dressed in clothes halfway between demure and flapper. Their names are DINAH and JENNIE. BUGSY takes DINAH's arm and kisses her on the cheek. She is clearly his girl. MEYER smiles at JENNIE and hands her a flower. She smiles back shyly.

JENNIE
>Thanks.

BUGSY
>C'mon lovebirds, yer holdin' up the parade!

He grabs MEYER by the shoulder and propels him out the door.

CUT TO

INT. DANCE HALL - NIGHT

A black SINGER stands on a makeshift stage. Behind him is a large banner reading: "DELANCY STREET DANCE -BROOKLYN, NEW YORK." A small jazz combo stands ready to play.

SINGER
>I said its hot time! Its swing time! Its let's hear it time!

The room explodes with applause. We PULL BACK and see that it is a dingy auditorium filled to the rafters with young Jewish kids, dressed up for the occasion. A cloud of cigarette smoke hangs over the crowd. The band erupts into song, playing a furious hot jazz tune. The crowd begins to dance.

The boys are coming in with their dates. MEYER and BUGSY and LEPKE and MOESY and DUTCH, all decked out for the occasion. They are beginning to look prosperous. LEPKE sports a gold watch on a chain. MOESY is wearing an expensive suit with a vest. Heads turn as they enter.

BUGSY
>Now, remember, these are nice girls, so behave yourself.

MEYER

    Me?

BUGSY

    Well, remind me to behave myself.

He flips DINAH around and kisses her on the mouth. She laughs and pushes him away.

MEYER

    Behave yourself, you fuckin' animal.

BUGSY

    Thanks, little man.

LEPKE

    Holy shit.

BUGSY

    What?

LEPKE

    Take a look at who we got here.

THEIR POV of a tall, older man walking through the crowd. People are greeting him politely, even deferentially. He is dressed in an impeccably clean white suit. A gold watch chain is slung around his waistcoat. A white fedora hat sits perched on his head.

JOEY LEVINE emerges from the crowd with his boys. The man takes him by the shoulder and begins talking to him. LEVINE nods with a worried look on his face. The man's name, we will learn, is legendary.

He is ARNOLD ROTHSTEIN, businessman, gambler extraordinaire, king of the Jewish underworld.

BUGSY

    Holy shit. It's Rothstein.

MEYER

    Who's Rothstein?

LEPKE

    Rothstein? Little man, Rothstein is the name of a king. The one Jew even the eye-talians won't touch.

BUGSY

    That's him kid. Biggest gambler ever walked the earth. You think you got brains kid? You're lookin' at the smartest fuckin' Jew in America.

DUTCH

    Looks like him and Levine got business.

BUGSY

    Yeah. Not for long though.

LEVINE gestures towards the boys. ROTHSTEIN looks up, glances at them and goes back to speaking with LEVINE.

DINAH
      C'mon Benny, let's dance.

BUGSY smiles.

BUGSY
      She's right, this aint a night for business.

They head out on to the dance floor and join the dancing crowd.

                    FADE TO

LATER

A slow, bluesy number is being played. Couples dance close, grinding together provocatively. The lights are low. It is very, very late.

We TRACK SLOWLY through the crowd. Past MEYER and JENNIE, who are kissing passionately. We STOP on BUGSY and DINAH. They are dancing close, but with a distant, chaste feeling about them.

DINAH
      You know, Benny, a lot of people warned me about you.

BUGSY
      Oh, yeah?

DINAH
      Yeah. They said you were a tough kid. That you were mean and low and that... You like
      to hurt people. But you're not so bad.

BUGSY smiles his big, toothy smile.

BUGSY
      You're wrong, honey. I'm worse.

She looks up at him, confused, as if she doesn't know if he's joking or not. Someone taps on BUGSY's shoulder. He lets DINAH go and turns around. It's JOEY LEVINE.

LEVINE
      How you doin', Bugsy?

BUGSY pushes DINAH aside.

BUGSY
      Who you talkin' to, Levine?

LEVINE
      I'm talkin' to you, Bugs.

BUGSY
      I am not a bug, you cocksucker. I am not a fucking insect.

LEVINE

Stay away from my fuckin' marks you hebe piece of shit. You and the rest of your faggot crew.

BUGSY
Fuck you, Levine. We're the game now, not you.

A crowd begins to gather around them. The boys try to elbow through.

LEVINE
They're right about you, Bugsy. You're a certee-fied nutcase. Do you know who you're fucking with here?

He barely finishes the sentence. BUGSY PUNCHES HIM IN THE FACE with terrific force.

LEVINE's nose EXPLODES in a gout of blood. The music stops dead. LEVINE falls to the floor, holding his nose.

BUGSY lunges forward, but MOESY and DUTCH hold him back.

MEYER watches. He's worried. Things are getting out of control.

There is a terrible, pregnant silence. Finally, LEVINE climbs back onto his feet. He lets his nose bleed down his cheek and on to his shirt collar.

BUGSY strains to attack LEVINE again. The boys hold him back.

One of LEVINE's boys grabs LEVINE's arm to pull him away. LEVINE's eyes level on DINAH.

CLOSE UP of DINAH, looking bewildered at the sudden turn of events.

CLOSE UP of LEVINE. His eyes are shadowed. There is something dark and terrible in them. He thinks he sees BUGSY's weakness.

LEVINE takes a handkerchief from his pocket and wipes his nose. He turns the bloodstained handkerchief over in his hand. BUGSY glowers at him.

LEVINE
Next time I see you, Bugs, I'll kill you.

BUGSY
Anytime you say.

OVERHEAD SHOT of LEVINE's boys as they pull him away and out of the room. MOESY and DUTCH release BUGSY. He doesn't move a muscle. He stands stock still in the middle of the room. His fists are still clenched together. The band starts up the music again.

                                                            FADE TO

INT. SIEGEL APARTMENT - NIGHT

It is the small hours of the morning. The boys are seated around the cramped kitchen table. MOESY is wrapping up BUGSY's fist. BUGSY has a cigarette hanging from the corner of his mouth. They speak in low voices.

BUGSY

I think I broke a fuckin' knuckle on that mamzer's nose.

MOESY

Nah, Ben. You can still move your fingers. You just banged it up a little.

BUGSY

Sonofabitch. I'm gonna kill that motherfucker. I swear to God.

MEYER

Benny, you gotta lay low on this one. Half a Brooklyn saw you break Levine's nose. If he gets hit by a car on 5th Street they're gonna come lookin' for you.

BUGSY

Meyer, will you stop thinking for five minutes. This fucker drew a line. Do you understand?

MEYER

No, he told us something.

BUGSY

What?

DUTCH

Meyer, you got to talk a little more straight.

MEYER

He sent us a message tonight.

BUGSY

Oh yeah? I didn't get it.

MEYER

He's scared.

Pause.

BUGSY

So what? So he's scared.

MEYER

People make mistakes when they're scared.

DUTCH

Meyer, this little shit threw down on Benny. That's a fuckin' challenge. Either we answer or we look like jokers.

MEYER

What are you gonna do? We're gonna kill a guy connected with Rothstein? With Marranzano? With the Moustache Petes in Manhattan? Just like that? You think these bastards would think twice about cuttin' our throats?

BUGSY

So what do we do? Nothing?

MEYER

That's right. Nothing. He's scared. He's gonna fuck up. We wait until he does. Then we move. But not before.

Silence.

LEPKE

I hate to say this, but it makes sense.

BUGSY

Shut the fuck up, Louie.

DUTCH

No, he's right Benny. We aint got nothin' like the muscle to take on a Manhattan guy.

BUGSY

Aw, shit. I was looking forward to killin' that motherfucker.

He stubs out the cigarette on the table with his free hand.

BUGSY

Sometimes, little man, you're too fuckin' smart for your own good.

FADE TO

EXT. STREET - EVENING

DINAH comes out of the door of her father's clothing shop. The sign in Yiddish and English reads: "EPSTEIN'S FINE GARMENTS." JENNIE is waiting for her.

ALL OF THE FOLLOWING IS A SINGLE SHOT:

The two girls walk down the street, talking and giggling. They turn a corner, and head down a darker, less populated side street. Suddenly, they stop.

We SWING AROUND and see JOEY LEVINE standing before them. His nose is swaddled in an enormous white bandage. It gives him a grotesque, monstrous look.

The girls begin to back up slowly. But LEVINE's boys are behind them. One of them grabs JENNIE, putting his hand over her mouth. She squirms and tries to scream. LEVINE's boys hold her fast while LEVINE pulls DINAH by the arm into a nearby alley.

We FOLLOW THEM as LEVINE pushes DINAH against a pile of refuse and starts ripping at her clothes. DINAH screams. LEVINE hits her in the face. Several of his boys hold her down while he rips her clothes.

We slowly TRACK BACKWARDS out of the alley and back down the street. Past JENNIE and the boys who are holding her. Past the turn into the back street. Out into the bustling thoroughfare as we slowly...

FADE TO

INT. EPSTEIN APARTMENT - NIGHT

DINAH is asleep in bed. White pillows are drawn up around her. The blanket pulled up to her neck. She has a black eye and a swollen lip. Her face is cut and bruised.

Slowly, the door to the bedroom is closed. The black shadow covers DINAH's face as we...

CUT TO

BUGSY closing the door. He walks back into:

INT. THE EPSTEIN KITCHEN - NIGHT

BUGSY stands in the doorway. His hands are in his pockets.

CLOSE UP of JENNIE. She is sitting in a chair, sniffling. Her eyes and cheeks are red from crying.

CLOSE UP of DINAH'S PARENTS. Her mother is quietly weeping. DINAH's father's arms are around her.

CLOSE UP of BUGSY. His eyes are icy cold, almost receding back into his head.

CLOSE UP of MEYER. His hands are on JENNIE's shoulders. He looks up at BUGSY. The look on his face is half shame and half fear.

CLOSE UP of BUGSY. His lips are set. His face like stone. Something in him looks terrifying, murderous.

CUT TO

INT. BUTCHER'S SHOP - NIGHT

LENNY AARONSOHN, clad in a white butcher's apron, is removing cuts of meat from the display counter.

THE FOLLOWING IS A SINGLE SHOT:

LENNY walks into the back room where his father, DAVID, is taking stock.

LENNY
        You want these in the freezer, Pop?

DAVID
        You bring the cutlets too?

LENNY
        No, you want the cutlets?

DAVID
        Of course! They spoil the fastest! How you gonna run this business if you don't
        remember these things?

LENNY doesn't answer.

DAVID

Go put them away.

We follow LENNY as he goes into the freezer room. Great slabs of frozen meat hang on hooks from the ceiling. He mutters to himself under his breath as he puts the cuts of meat on a rack and wipes his hands on his apron. He walks out of the freezer and closes the heavy door behind him. As he turns, he stops dead in his tracks.

We SWING AROUND and see LENNY's father standing in the corner. MOESY and DUTCH are holding guns to his head. LEPKE stands by the door with MEYER, blocking the only exit. Standing in the center of the room, his arms stiff at his sides, hands curled up into fists, is BUGSY SIEGEL.

BUGSY
        (very quiet) Siddown, Lenny.

LENNY doesn't move a muscle.

DAVID
        Lenny, who are these boys?

BUGSY
        SHUT UP OLD MAN!!!

LENNY is still frozen solid in his place. BUGSY nods to LEPKE, who crosses the room and grabs LENNY by the shoulder. He drags him across the room and pushes him down in a seat at the cutting table. LEPKE hold him there, one hand on his shoulder. BUGSY sits down on the edge of the table.

BUGSY
        Where is he, Lenny?

LENNY
        Benny, I don't know who you're talkin' about...

BUGSY PUNCHES HIM IN THE FACE. He almost falls out of his chair but LEPKE pulls him back up.

DAVID
        Lenny!

BUGSY
        I SAID SHUT UP! DON'T MAKE ME SAY IT AGAIN!

He turns back to LENNY. A slow trickle of blood runs down from LENNY's nose.

BUGSY
        Where is he, Lenny?

LENNY
        Benny, I... I don't know where he is...

BUGSY PUNCHES HIM AGAIN. One of LENNY'S teeth goes flying out. He spits up a gout of blood and coughs. LEPKE holds him firmly in place.

LENNY
        Benny... Benny... I can't... he'll kill me...

BUGSY
  It's me you got to worry about right now, Lenny. Where is he?

LENNY starts to blubber incoherently, shaking his head from side to side.

LENNY
  I can't...I can't...

BUGSY walks over to a rack of tools against the far wall. He looks it over, then picks something off and comes back to the table. He places a large meat cleaver on the cutting table.

BUGSY
  Hold him, Lepkele.

LEPKE grabs LENNY's hand and slams it down flat on the table. BUGSY picks up the cleaver.

BUGSY
  I'm gonna give you to the count of three to tell me where that motherfucker is. Then I'm gonna start cutting your fat fingers off.

LENNY starts to cry.

BUGSY
  One.

LENNY
  NO, BENNY, PLEASE!!!

BUGSY
  Two.

LENNY starts to scream incoherently.

DAVID
  For God's sake, Lenny! Tell him what he wants to know!

BUGSY
  THREE!

HE SLAMS DOWN THE CLEAVER. A blast of blood SPATTERS against the wall. LENNY shrieks like a wounded animal. LEPKE holds him tight in his chair.

LENNY
  Alright! Alright! (He begins to weep uncontrollably, like a child.) I'll tell you... I'll tell you...

BUGSY nods. LEPKE lets LENNY go. LENNY cradles his mutilated hand and begins to wail uncontrollably. Blood pours out over his knuckles.

We CLOSE IN to a CLOSE UP of BUGSY. His eyes are like black ice.

BUGSY
  WHERE?!!!

                                                                    CUT TO

EXT. GOLDMAN'S CAFE - NIGHT

A flash of lightning ON THE CUT illuminates a sign: "GOLDMAN'S CAFE - CLOSED FOR THE NIGHT". A furious downpour is sending sheets of rain down on to the jagged streets and half-ruined sidewalks. There is a clap of thunder.

We MOVE THROUGH the rain soaked window and...

DISSOLVE TO

INT. GOLDMAN'S CAFE - NIGHT

We TRACK SLOWLY through the darkened cafe. Chairs are stacked up on tables. The bar is cleared. In the back, we see a faint glow. As we GET CLOSER, we see JOEY LEVINE and STAN GOLDMAN --the owner of the bar --playing cards at a small table. It is lit by a tiny electric lamp. LEVINE slams down a hand and smiles.

LEVINE
        Gin! Cards aint with you tonight, is they Stan?

GOLDMAN
        I guess not. Shit. How much I owe you?

LEVINE
        I'll settle for five, considering your hospitality.

GOLDMAN throws a bill on the table and gets up.

GOLDMAN
        I gotta take a piss.

He disappears down a narrow corridor behind the bar.

We move in CLOSER on LEVINE. He is shuffling the cards. There is another lightning flash. LEVINE taps the edge of the deck against the table. There is a clap of thunder. LEVINE looks up, nervous. He places the cards neatly on the table.

There is a SHARP NOISE. He looks up again. CLOSE UP of LEVINE. He is listening intently for another sound. There is nothing except the rain pattering on the roof. He gets up, pushing the table away from him.

LEVINE
        Stan?

Pause.

LEVINE
        Stan, you fall in or something?

Nothing. Gingerly, LEVINE walks behind the bar and looks down the corridor. Again nothing. LEVINE walks down the corridor and knocks on the bathroom door.

LEVINE

Stan? You in there?

No answer. He tries to open the door. It's locked. Slowly, LEVINE begins to back away. Then he turns and hurries out into the bar. He stops, a shocked look on his face. BUGSY SIEGEL is seated at the table. Behind him stand MEYER, MOESY and DUTCH. LEVINE turns to run, but LEPKE is standing behind him in the shadows.

CLOSE UP of BUGSY. His eyes are like knife blades. LEVINE stands frozen in place. BUGSY picks a whiskey bottle off the table and pours two shots.

CLOSE UP of the SHOT GLASS. With a single, steady finger BUGSY slides it over to the other side of the table. LEVINE nervously sits down across from BUGSY. He looks up anxiously at LEPKE looming above him.

CLOSE UP of BUGSY. He says nothing. He looks completely calm. He doesn't move a muscle.

His hand shaking, LEVINE picks up the shot glass and downs it. He wipes his mouth with his sleeve.

LEVINE
        Look, Benny...

BUGSY SMASHES HIM ACROSS THE FACE with the whiskey bottle. LEVINE careens over on to the floor. BUGSY bounds to his feet and starts brutally kicking LEVINE. LEVINE shrieks with a high-pitched, feminine scream that is horrifying to hear.

His face contorted by rage, BUGSY picks up a chair and smashes LEVINE over the head with it over and over again. The chair begins to fly to pieces. BUGSY lets out a ferocious, animal scream from the back of his throat. His face is speckled with LEVINE's blood.

CLOSE UP of MEYER. He is half in shadow. There is a look of horror on his face.

LEPKE lays his hand on BUGSY's shoulder. BUGSY looks up, breathing hard, his eyes afire. A trickle of blood, not his own, runs down his cheek.

CLOSE UP of LEPKE. He looks calmly at BUGSY.

BUGSY lets the remains of the chair drop from his hands. He wipes the blood from his face with his sleeve. LEVINE is inert, motionless on the floor.

We begin to PULL BACK. BUGSY takes a revolver from his belt and fires two shots point-blank into LEVINE. The shots light up the room with a terrible white light.

CLOSE UP of MEYER. He flinches at the sound of the explosions.

CLOSE UP of BUGSY IN PROFILE. He is spent. Slowly, his breathing returns to normal. The light from the window throws the shadows of raindrops on to his face. They roll down his cheek like tears.

Slowly, the boys begin to leave the darkened bar. BUGSY spits on LEVINE's corpse. LEPKE takes his arm and pulls him away.

                                                              CUT TO

EXT. GOLDMAN'S CAFE - NIGHT

The door with the hanging sign: "GOLDMAN'S CAFE - CLOSED FOR THE NIGHT" opens and the boys come out one by one. OVERHEAD SHOT of the boys slowly making their way off through the driving rain.

                                                    CUT TO

INT. JUDY'S WHOREHOUSE - DAY

LENNY AARONSOHN, his hand wrapped in a thick bandage, black eye turning green, is sitting across from BUGSY, surrounded by LEVINE's boys. BUGSY taps the end of a cigarette lighter on the table. The sound is excruciating to LENNY. The tension is becoming unbearable. BUGSY stops tapping.

BUGSY
        When you want to do it?

LENNY
        Tonight. The alley beside Seidmann's.

BUGSY nods.

LENNY
        Blades and bats only.

BUGSY
        You got it.

LENNY gets up awkwardly. He and his boys file out of the bar. BUGSY lights a cigarette.

BUGSY
        How many can we raise?

MEYER
        Twenty. Maybe twenty-five.

BUGSY nods.

BUGSY
        That'll have to be enough.

                                                    CUT TO

EXT. ALLEY - NIGHT

It is pouring rain again, a ferocious April downpour. We see a large sign, "SEIDMANN'S DISCOUNT WAREHOUSE." We begin to PULL BACK. Out of the bottom of the frame come LENNY and the remnants of LEVINE's crew. Their collars turned up and caps pulled down. Several of them are toting large pieces of wood and long crowbars. One of them twirls a knife between his fingers.

OVERHEAD SHOT of them as they make their way to the dark alley next to the warehouse.

Slowly, from the shadows and dark corners come their enemies, carrying weapons of every imaginable description; steak knives and rotting boards, old baseball bats and fireplace pokers. In the center of them are BUGSY, MEYER and the boys, who stride purposely out into the center of the alley as the rain spatters into the overflowing gutters and sends spurts of water into the air, illuminated in the auburn streetlights.

BUGSY and LENNY face off.

BUGSY
    I'm ready when you are Aaronsohn.

LENNY steps forward and draws a long butcher's knife from his belt. In a swift movement, he cuts the sling around his shoulder and lets his bandaged hand fall free.

LENNY
    You had this comin' for a long time, Bugs.

BUGSY
    I got a name, Aaronsohn.

LENNY
    You're an insect, Bugs. That's all you'll ever be.

BUGSY pulls a long switchblade from his pocket and spits into the street in front of LENNY. LENNY begins to advance towards him.

CLOSE UP of MEYER. He pulls a short crowbar from his belt.

BUGSY AND LENNY slowly circle each other. The rain pounds down. Nobody moves. The tension is excruciating.

LENNY swipes at BUGSY who dodges. Everyone gasps, but no one moves a muscle.

CLOSE UP of BUGSY. He has his icy look again as he circles. He seems terrifyingly calm.

LENNY lunges again and misses. BUGSY steps aside and slashes LENNY's cheek. LENNY bounds backward, knocking against the alley wall, holding his cheek in his hand.

CLOSE UP of BUGSY. He smiles.

LENNY yells and hacks crazily at BUGSY, who half-turns and catches the blow on his upper arm. A red slash glows crimson in the rain.

CLOSE UP of BUGSY's feet. Tiny drops of blood fall to the pavement and are washed away.

BUGSY steps back and braces himself. For a moment, they circle each other again. Then LENNY lunges forward. BUGSY catches him and stabs him twice in the side. It all happens in a split-second. We barely see it. LENNY stumbles out of BUGSY's grip. The blood and rain run down BUGSY's arm. LENNY looks up, holding his side. The rain tumbles down his face. Blood runs through his fingers. The shot TILTS slightly on its axis. LENNY collapses into the street. There is a long, terrible silence. LENNY does not move. The rain pours down, washing the blood into the gutter.

Suddenly, in a rush of movement, LEVINE's boys rush forward, and the scene becomes a furious, no holds barred street fight between the narrow alley walls.

BUGSY stabs another of LEVINE's boys. A boy is thrown into a pile of garbage cans. LEPKE smashes someone over the head with a bat, crushing his skull in a spurt of blood and bone.

CLOSE UP of MEYER. Momentarily frozen.

A group of boys furiously beat a prostrate figure.

DUTCH is tackled by two boys.

MEYER suddenly comes to his senses and starts beating them with his crowbar. A body falls into the rain-swept street.

Fists fly. Legs run and crumple underneath the crush.

Shadows of the battling figures are thrown against the alley wall by the streetlight.

OVERHEAD SHOT of the battle in full scale, a horrifying mosaic of slamming weapons and pummeled bodies.

CLOSE UP of BUGSY. His face is contorted with monstrous rage.

A boy tries to crawl away from the carnage.

There is a sudden flurry of shouting voices. The boys begin to run, disappearing down the sidestreets and doorways.

OVERHEAD SHOT of BUGSY standing triumphant in the middle of the street as the last of LEVINE's boys flee the scene, beaten.

We hear the high-pitched blast of a police whistle. MEYER grabs BUGSY by the shoulder.

MEYER
        Benny! Benny it's the cops! We gotta go!

BUGSY says nothing. He is breathing hard, the rain running down his dirty face.

MEYER
        Benny, c'mon!

Behind them, the boys are scattering in all directions.

Slowly, BUGSY turns his head to look at MEYER.

CLOSE UP of BUGSY. He takes a deep breath and closes his eyes. The rain runs down his face, washing away the blood of his victims. He is no longer a punk. He is a king.

CUT TO

INT. OFFICE - DAY

ARNOLD ROTHSTEIN is reclining in an easy chair, a long cigar between his fingers. He takes a puff and blows a plume of smoke into the air.

The boys are seated uncomfortably on the plush office furniture. BUGSY's arm is in a sling. DUTCH has a prominent bandage on his face and MOESY sports a black eye. They look nervous.

CLOSE UP of ROTHSTEIN. He taps some ash on to the floor.

ROTHSTEIN

I've always said that honesty is the most important thing about running a dishonest business. So, I'm gonna be straight with you boys. You done me no good with this bullshit. Steccio and Maranzano don't got the patience for this kind of nonsense. The way you boys have been fuckin' things up lately, I shoulda rubbed out the buncha you a week ago.

MEYER

But that wouldn't be the smart thing, would it Mr. Rothstein?

ROTHSTEIN

Excuse me, young fella?

MEYER

The smart thing to do is wait. Don't fly off the handle. Maybe we're better than Joey Levine and his crew. Maybe we're smarter, maybe we're stronger. Why not wait to find out who comes out on top?

ROTHSTEIN

What's your name, son?

MEYER

Meyer Lansky.

ROTHSTEIN

Well, Meyer Lansky, shut the fuck up while I'm talking. (To everyone:) Now, basically, what your little friend here is saying is essentially accurate.

BUGSY looks confused.

ROTHSTEIN

That means he's right.

BUGSY

Yeah, well, the little man's the one with the brains in this outfit.

ROTHSTEIN

Yeah, I can see that. (Pause) Now, you boys have caused me a lotta fuckin' trouble the last few days. It's all I could do to keep the Pete's from cuttin' your throats over this meshugas.

DUTCH

Fuckin' wops.

They all laugh, except for ROTHSTEIN.

ROTHSTEIN

You want to be something in this town, son, you're gonna learn to watch what you say.

There is an embarrassed silence.

ROTHSTEIN

Even amongst friends. (Pause) But, there's somethin' to be said for the enthusiasm of youth. I know hutzpah when I see it. And you kids look like you been buyin' it wholesale.

BUGSY

Alright, Mr. Rothstein. Lets get down to it, ok?

MEYER

Shut up, Benny. Let him talk.

BUGSY looks angrily at MEYER.

ROTHSTEIN

(To BUGSY:) Listen to your friend, kid. He's a talker. Talkers always win in the end.

MEYER

He's right, though, Mr. Rothstein. What's in it for us?

ROTHSTEIN

A foot in the door. I know people who know people. People what could use a couple of shitkicking punks like you.

MEYER

We aint errand boys, Mr. Rothstein.

BUGSY

That's right. Whatever we get into, we want a piece of it. Upfront.

ROTHSTEIN

Let me tell you boys about the future. You ever hear of Prohibition?

DUTCH

You mean the Drys?

ROTHSTEIN

That's right.

BUGSY

(Laughing) What, Brooklyn's gonna go dry?

They laugh.

ROTHSTEIN

Not just Brooklyn, kid. The whole country.

BUGSY

Bullshit.

ROTHSTEIN

The details won't mean nothin' to you. But take my word for it. In a year, this whole country will be dry. No liquor no place. The demon rum is gonna be 100% illegal.

BUGSY

That's crazy.

DUTCH

Hell yeah it's crazy.

ROTHSTEIN

It's not crazy, kid. It's happening. Fifteen states already got it on the books, another five before the year is out. But it won't matter by that time. It'll be in the Constitution by then.

BUGSY

Gonna be rough on the rummys.

They laugh.

ROTHSTEIN

It's gonna be rough on a lot of folks.

BUGSY

I think I'm missin' something.

ROTHSTEIN

Tell me somethin' kid. You think when that law goes on the books, folks are just gonna stop drinkin'?

MEYER

No.

BUGSY

What do you mean no? Where they gonna get the stuff?

MEYER

From us.

CLOSE UP CLOSING IN on ROTHSTEIN. He is smiling.

ROTHSTEIN

Smart kid. Smart kid. (He puffs on his cigar.) From us.

BUGSY

What are you talkin' about? Where we gonna get it?

ROTHSTEIN

Buy it, make it, run it in from Canada, who cares? Getting it's the easy part.

BUGSY

What's the hard part?

ROTHSTEIN

First of all, getting it to places it can be sold at a...let's say a substantial markup. Second, shall we say, eliminating the competition. And third: figuring out what to do with all the money we're gonna make.

MEYER

"We," Mr. Rothstein?

ROTHSTEIN

That's up to you.

CUT TO

EXT. SHORE OF LAKE ERIE - NIGHT

The boys are standing by a truck, looking cold and unhappy. A boat dock sits empty at the end of a short path in front of them. BUGSY stamps his feet to keep warm. MEYER is looking out on to the lake. He has a clipboard tucked under his arm.

BUGSY
I hate the fuckin' cold. I ever tell you that?

MEYER
All the time, Benny. All the time.

BUGSY
Yeah, well, it's true. I hate this weather. (He blows on his hands.) If you ask me, hell aint burnin' hot, its freezin' fuckin' cold.

DUTCH
Alright Benny, it's cold, we gotcha.

BUGSY
I'm just sayin...

MEYER
Benny, let it go.

BUGSY
I'm just sayin' I can understand why they usually send Italians to do this kinda work. I mean, they're used to this kind of weather.

MEYER
Benny, Italy's a hot country.

BUGSY
You sure about that?

MEYER
Yeah, Benny, I'm sure.

BUGSY
Yeah, well, I'm still freezin' my ass off.

DUTCH
We got it, Benny, we got it.

BUGSY
Oh, the Dutchman speaks!

MEYER
Here he comes.

They hear the noise of a boat engine far off in the distance. BUGSY suddenly becomes serious; he pulls a long-barreled shotgun from under his jacket and hops on to the hood of the truck. MEYER walks to the boat dock, DUTCH and LEPKE follow him. MOESY gets behind the wheel of the truck and turns on the headlights.

From out in the center of the lake, a large speedboat approached, a single yellow lantern hanging from its windshield. The engine cuts and it glides slowly into the dock. The CAPTAIN, a stocky Irishman in a wool hat, throws a rope to DUTCH, who looks at it quizzically.

CAPTAIN
        Tie it to the dock, city boy!

DUTCH ties it to the dock. The CAPTAIN steps on to the dock.

CAPTAIN
        You the new fellas?

MEYER holds out his hand.

MEYER
        Yeah. I'm Meyer Lansky.

The CAPTAIN does not shake it.

CAPTAIN
        What, they sendin' me hebes now?

BUGSY cocks his shotgun.

BUGSY
        Watch your fuckin' mouth!

The CAPTAIN squints in the glare of the headlights, trying to see who it is.

MEYER
        You better watch out for Benny, he's the crazy type.

CAPTAIN
        More fuckin' trouble then I need. Let's get down to business.

MEYER
        It's all here?

The CAPTAIN reaches down and pulls a tarpaulin off the back of the boat. Underneath it are two dozen large wooden vats.

CAPTAIN
        Twenty-four kegs of genuine Canadian whiskey. Turn the hair on the devil's ass white.

MEYER
        Good.

He beckons the truck forward. BUGSY hops off and the truck begins rolling forward.

                                                    CUT TO

LATER

DUTCH and MOESY push the last keg into the truck, slamming the back shut. MEYER hands the CAPTAIN a large wad of bills. He counts them nonchalantly.

CAPTAIN
    Just a formality. I know you people are good with numbers.

BUGSY
    Hey, how do we know you didn't dip into some of that hootch yourself? I heard you micks got a taste for it.

The CAPTAIN looks daggers at him, and then puts the bills into his jacket pocket.

CAPTAIN
    (To MEYER) Tell your friend to watch his mouth. It'll get him in trouble one day.

MEYER
    He can take care of himself.

CAPTAIN
    Yeah, sure.

He gets back on the boat and starts the engine. MEYER undoes the rope and tosses it into the boat. It backs slowly out of the dock and speeds away, becoming nothing more than a speck of light on the horizon.

MEYER
    Alright, let's get this stuff outta here.

BUGSY
    Thank fuckin' God.

They clamber into the truck.

FADE TO

INT. TRUCK - NIGHT

BUGSY is driving, MEYER seated next to him, looking over his clipboard. MOESY and DUTCH are sleeping on top of the vats in the back. LEPKE is perched on top of one, smoking a cigarette.

BUGSY
    Hand me a smoke, will you little man?

MEYER gives him a cigarette. BUGSY lights it one handed with a gleaming silver lighter, obviously newly acquired.

BUGSY
    Fuckin' micks. I hate those drunk cocksuckers.

MEYER
    Those drunk cocksuckers are makin' us rich.

BUGSY

Yeah, well... I'm just sayin', they're a buncha drunks and we're gettin' rich sellin' 'em the booze.

MEYER

'Cos us people are good with numbers?

BUGSY

You know what I'm talkin' about Meyer. Wouldn't catch no Jew stuffin' his face with scotch at two in the afternoon. That's all I'm sayin...

MEYER

It's just business, Benny, that's all. It's just dollars and cents, aint nothin' more than that.

BUGSY

You think too much, little man, I ever tell you that?

MEYER

All the time.

BUGSY

Thinkin' aint a bad thing, I aint sayin' that. Its thinkin' that keeps a man outta the gutter. But thinkin' aint nuthin' without a gun and a blade behind it. That's the truth of the thing, little man.

MEYER

Benny, what the fuck are you talkin' about?

BUGSY

Nothin. Forget it...

MEYER

Good.

He closes his eyes and starts to doze.

BUGSY

What the fuck is this?

REVERSE SHOT THROUGH THE WINDSHIELD: We see lights shining in the middle of the road. Slowly, we see two cars blocking the road and men toting shotguns advancing on them.

MEYER

Shit.

BUGSY brings the truck to a halt.

BUGSY

Moe, Dutch, Louie! We got trouble!

The boys in the back scramble to find their weapons. BUGSY pulls the emergency break and grabs a shotgun from under his seat. MEYER grabs his arm.

MEYER

Benny! We talk first, you understand!

BUGSY looks at him for a moment, then nods.

BUGSY

Alright, we play it your way, but if these fuckers start anything I'm gonna saw 'em in half.

CUT TO

EXT. HIGHWAY - NIGHT

MEYER and BUGSY climb out of the truck, its lights still burning, casting beams across the empty street. BUGSY's shotgun hangs loose at his side. One of the men walks forward into the glare of the headlights. It is LUCKY LUCIANO.

LUCKY

Out late tonight, boys?

BUGSY

What do you want?

LUCKY

Steccio wants his booze.

BUGSY

Tell him he can shove it up his greaseball ass and set fire to it.

MEYER

Benny, wait a minute!

LUCKY turns to MEYER and recognizes him.

LUCKY

How you doin' kid? How's the eye?

MEYER

Better every day.

LUCKY

Glad to hear it.

BUGSY

You know this joker, Meyer?

LUCKY

We met in passing.

MEYER

Somethin' like that.

LUCKY

Small world, aint it?

MEYER

Tell me about it.

LUCKY

It's a shame business has to interfere with these happy reunions.

MEYER

Aint it though?

BUGSY

What the fuck is goin' on here?

MEYER

Tell Steccio he'll get his like always. If he don't like it, he can talk to Rothstein.

LUCKY

I don't answer to no Rothstein. Far as I'm concerned, Steccio is law round here, and Steccio wants his booze.

BUGSY

Why don't he come over here and get it then?

He slaps his shotgun into the palm of his hand. DUTCH appears on the roof of the truck, cocking a rifle. LUCKY's men go for the weapons in their pockets.

MEYER

Wait! Wait! (To LUCKY) Listen to me! Nobody's got to answer to nobody right now!

LUCKY

What?

MEYER

Right now there aint no Steccio, and there aint no Rothstein. I don't see 'em here, do you?

LUCKY

Stand aside little man.

MEYER

It's just us here. We're just talkin'. And aint nobody got to die tonight if we don't want it.

LUCKY looks over at BUGSY, who lowers his weapon slightly.

MEYER

Now whatever's goin' on here, it's between Rothstein and Steccio, not us. I say we let them kill each other if they want. But me, I want to stay walkin' tonight.

LUCKY thinks it over for a minute.

LUCKY

What about me? I gotta have something to show for all this.

MEYER

Twenty percent.

BUGSY

What?!

MEYER

Twenty percent.

LUCKY says nothing.

MEYER

> We shoot it out now, that means a war, and that means nobody earns. We go in together, everyone takes a little less, but everyone comes out on top in the end.

There is a long pause. BUGSY's fingers twitch nervously on the barrel of his gun. LUCKY scratches his cheek and turns back to his men.

LUCKY

> Let 'em through, boys!

MEYER exhales. BUGSY lowers his weapon. DUTCH jumps off the roof of the truck. They clamber back in and drive off through the roadblock.

CUT TO

INT. ROTHSTEIN'S OFFICE - DAY

It is a fashionable New York hotel suite. ROTHSTEIN is seated behind a mahogany desk leaden with papers; smoking one of his ubiquitous cigars. The boys are assembled around him.

ROTHSTEIN

> You boys did the right thing. There's no profit in shootin' it out with the wops on their own territory. Goddam fuckin' Steccio. He's got Maranzano breathing up his ass, so he's crackin' the whip on everybody, tryin' to show 'em who's boss. (Pause) This whole thing could blow up any day now.

CUT TO

EXT. STECCIO'S MANSION - DAY

STECCIO, a tall, thin man with gray hair and a face criss-crossed by scars and wrinkles, is walking with LUCKY through his garden. It is the garden of a newly rich man, complete with fountain and marble statues. Several gardeners are working in the background.

STECCIO

> These fuckin' Jews. Lend 'em a dime, you get three cents back, if you're lucky! They are not like us. I tell you, Salvatore, blood is everything. You can only trust your own, and even then, you have to be careful. My grandfather, he was a great man in the old country, he never made a deal with anyone who didn't have the same last name as him. He told me: "Antonio, only one thing in life is certain, a Sicilian never spills the blood of his brother, because it's like spilling his own." Remember that.

LUCKY

> I will.

STECCIO

> Well, you did the right thing. No one wants a war right now. We'll deal with these...Hebrews...when the time comes.

CUT TO

INT. ROTHSTEIN'S OFFICE - DAY

ROTHSTEIN is leaning back in his leather chair; his eyes have a strange energy about them.

ROTHSTEIN

Yeah, he was great once. Meanest, most bloodthirsty sonofabitch ever walked the streets of Brooklyn. But now...he's an old man now. He's calcified. The world's changing and he don't even know it. Thinks he can live in his Sicilian cocoon for the next hundred years. To him, booze is just another run, just like women and cars and the crooked crap games. He doesn't see where it's going; where it can take us. The man is a goddam walking obstacle to progress. (Pause) What we could be, boys...with the right brains in the right suits and the right fingers on the trigger. (He laughs) Tony Steccio in his wildest wet dream couldn't imagine it. We could be bigger than the president of the United States if these fuckin' Moustache Pete's would get outta the way.

BUGSY

Maybe it's time we got 'em out of the way.

ROTHSTEIN

Didn't I tell you to learn to keep your mouth shut? Even amongst friends?

BUGSY

I didn't say nothin'.

ROTHSTEIN

Yeah, I didn't think you did. (Pause.) Sometimes a man says the most when he don't say nothin' at all.

                                                          CUT TO

EXT. STECCIO'S MANSION - DAY

STECCIO and LUCKY are standing before the ornate fountain.

STECCIO

I want you to stay close to these boys. See what you can find out about them.

LUCKY nods.

STECCIO

This guy Rothstein... he's smart, but he aint as smart as he thinks he is. These Jews, all they got is brains. But they got no loyalty. No loyalty even to their own blood. But they got brains, and that makes 'em dangerous. Rothstein thinks I'm on my way out. Thinks I'm goin' the way of the dodo. He's got no respect for steady things. Always lookin' for the future. The next angle. Sooner or later, he's gonna make his move. I wanna know when.

LUCKY

I'll get on it.

STECCIO grabs him by the shoulders and kisses him on the cheek.

STECCIO

You're a good boy Salvatore. I always said that. This boy, he's goin' places. Always said that.

They walk off towards the house.

CUT TO

INT. ROTHSTEIN'S OFFICE - DAY

ROTHSTEIN chews the end off another cigar and lights it.

ROTHSTEIN
I want you to stick close with this Luciano character. Steccio's got a way of doin' things, but maybe his younger guys don't.

MEYER
You think maybe he's got some boys that might not object to a change of hands?

ROTHSTEIN
Could be. The future is always with the young, aint that what they say every election day?

They all laugh.

ROTHSTEIN
Well, since you boys are workin' for me now, you're gonna have to start lookin' presentable.

BUGSY
What, I'm wearin' what I always wear.

ROTHSTEIN
Raw material, Benjamin, requires refining.

BUGSY looks at MEYER, wondering what the hell ROTHSTEIN is talking about.

CUT TO

INT. DEPARTMENT STORE - DAY

The boys are being outfitted by a group of tailors. ROTHSTEIN is watching the proceedings from an armchair, highly amused.

CLOSE UP of BUGSY. He looks down and smiles at the GIRL measuring his inner leg. She blushes.

CLOSE UP of LEPKE. He looks uncomfortable in a snappy white jacket.

CLOSE UP of MEYER. He looks at himself in the mirror, admiring his new fedora.

CUT TO

INT. BACK ROOM

The GIRL is going through some fabrics. BUGSY comes up behind her and whispers in her ear. She pushes him away, but she is smiling.

CUT TO

INT. DEPARTMENT STORE

ROTHSTEIN gestures his displeasure at MOESY's hat. The tailor replaces it with a darker one. ROTHSTEIN looks non-committal.

CLOSE UP of DUTCH. He looks at himself in the mirror, wearing the classic striped suit of the gangster, and smiles approvingly.

CUT TO

INT. BACKROOM

BUGSY and the MEASURING GIRL are fucking furiously on a sewing table amidst the rags and balls of thread.

CUT TO

INT. DEPARTMENT STORE

MEYER is looking at several ties in the mirror, trying to decide.

CLOSE UP of LEPKE. He looks at himself in his suit, which appears ill-fitting and awkward. It causes him to walk like a Frankenstein monster.

CLOSE UP of THE FOUR BOYS. They are framed in the same mirror, looking snazzy and dangerous. They are real gangsters now.

CLOSE UP of BUGSY emerging from the back room, tucking in his shirt. The boys look at him questioningly. He shrugs his shoulders and smirks.

CUT TO

INT. SPEAKEASY - NIGHT

A champagne cork pops and ROTHSTEIN pours out for the boys.

ROTHSTEIN
    To the spoils of war! To life! L'chaim!

EVERYONE
    L'chaim!

They all drink and throw their glasses against the wall.

WAITER
> More glasses, Mr. Rothstein?

ROTHSTEIN
> No, we're gonna pass the bottle.

WAITER
> More glasses.

He disappears into the crowd.

ROTHSTEIN
> Can't get good help these days.

They all laugh. The BOYS all have their girls with them. MEYER is with JENNY, who looks far more glamorous then when we last saw her.

ROTHSTEIN
> So come on, lovebirds, when's the big day?

JENNY
> Mr. Rothstein!

She blushes.

ROTHSTEIN
> Young lady, this man's going places! Catch him while you can!

Now MEYER is also blushing.

BUGSY
> Yeah, straight to Danamorra!

They all crack up laughing, except MEYER.

MEYER
> Benny, watch yourself, there's ladies present.

BUGSY
> Just jokin', little man, relax.

LEPKE
> Well, look what we got here.

Everyone turns to see what he is looking at. LUCKY LUCIANO emerges from the crowd.

LUCKY
> Evenin'.

ROTHSTEIN
> Good evening, young man.

LUCKY
> We've met, but we haven't really been introduced. I'm Salvatore Luciano. You can call me Lucky. I find folks of the Hebrew persuasion have trouble pronouncing my Christian name.

BUGSY

How about we call you Charlie? That's a nice name.

There are some chuckles around the table.

LUCKY

Whatever suits you. Mind if I join in?

MEYER

Business or pleasure?

LUCKY

Some of the one, most of the other.

Pause.

BUGSY

Girls, why don't take a trip to the powder room?

The girls get up to leave. JENNY looks to MEYER, who nods that she should go. LUCKY pulls out a seat next to ROTHSTEIN and sits down.

BUGSY

Alright, Charlie, what you got for us?

LUCKY

It's more like, what do we got for each other?

ROTHSTEIN

You're wasting our time, son.

LUCKY

Then I'll get to the point. Sometime this year Steccio and Marranzano are gonna shoot it out for who owns this city. Only one of 'em is gonna be left standin' when it's over.

MEYER

Tell us something we don't know.

LUCKY

What you don't know is that me and some of the other young guys might be of a certain mind about who we want to be standin'. As in, maybe we don't want neither one of 'em.

There is a pregnant silence.

MEYER

What's that got to do with us?

LUCKY

Maybe nothin', but the way I see it, all this shit about Italian territory and Jewish territory is nothin' but a waste of time and money. We aint livin' in the old country anymore. This is America, and we all stand to make a lot more money together then we do right now.

MEYER

You know the Moustache Petes'll never go along with that.

LUCKY

> Old men, little man. Still thinkin' like they did in them villages back in Sicily. Still thinkin' about blood instead of cash. In this country, blood don't mean shit. Cash does.

ROTHSTEIN

> And there are others in your organization who think like you do?

LUCKY

> I can't mention any names, you understand. If any of you was even a quarter Italian I wouldn't be sayin' any of this shit. But you folks got somethin' we don't.

BUGSY

> What's that?

LUCKY

> You don't live by the same rules. You don't play by the game of territories and families. You walk between the raindrops. Right now, neither of us can do shit, but together...

MEYER

> And if, by some amazing act of God, the Moustache Petes took an early retirement, you could get the other families to go along with this?

LUCKY

> The other families don't give a shit about nothin' except gettin' out from under Steccio's thumb. When the money starts rollin' in, they'll shut the fuck up pretty quick.

MEYER

> This is dangerous stuff you're talkin' about.

LUCKY

> Like I said, who are you guys gonna snitch to? Aint nobody on your side of the tracks that gives a shit.

MEYER

> Which is why you're coming to us in the first place.

LUCKY

> Yeah. That, and I seen you guys in action. You motherfuckers are as tough as any Italian I've ever seen and twice as smart.

BUGSY

> That's just Moesy here.

They all laugh.

LUCKY

> Think it over. You know where to find me.

He gets up, drinks down his glass of champagne and leaves. They all sit in silence for a moment, dumbfounded.

BUGSY

> What do you think Meyer?

MEYER looks at the table for a minute. Then he nods.

CUT TO

EXT. STECCIO'S GARDEN - DAY

STECCIO is watering his flowers. LUCKY is sitting on a bench nearby, smoking a cigarette and looking a little uncomfortable in the outdoor surroundings.

STECCIO

> I like to water the flowers. It relaxes me. My father, God rest his soul, used to have a garden back in the old country. Oh, he had boys who would tend the grass and things, but he always watered his own flowers. I asked him once why and he said: "It makes me feel like I'm not a tired old man anymore. It's the best way I know to lie to myself."

LUCKY chuckles politely.

STECCIO

> What did you find out?

LUCKY

> Not much. I think they're just punks that Rothstein's got under his wing. As long as he keeps payin' I don't think we got anything to worry about.

STECCIO

> Guy like Rothstein, there's always something to worry about. Man like that, always got an angle he's working.

LUCKY

> Maybe he's keeping one eye on Maranzano.

STECCIO

> Maranzano. That son of a Bronx whore. I shoulda finished him when I had the chance. He was always a bad one, you know, a bad seed! Never had no respect for nothin'!

LUCKY

> He's still movin' in on our Queens territories, and some in the Bronx too. Kicked the shit out of Four-Eyes Malloy a few weeks ago, aint heard a peep from the Micks since then.

STECCIO

> It's a sad thing, Salvatore.

He sits down painfully on the bench next to LUCKY.

STECCIO

> You know how I came to this country? A bum! Didn't have two cents to put together and now... (He gestures to the mansion and gardens) All this is mine. And more than that! I built this city, Salvatore! Everything we have: the politicians, the judges, the cops, down to the fifty-cent whores and the dollar speakeasies. La Cosa Nostra. I built it. And now... (He throws up his hands in a gesture of futility.) Now, the little fish start circling. They just want to take a bite, see what happens. Then another and another. Sooner or later... sooner or later you can feel yourself bleedin... (Pause.) I'm a tired old man, Salvatore. But I've got some blood in me still, and I want that cocksucker dead.

LUCKY

> No one wants a war, boss.

STECCIO

> Not yet they don't. Not yet they don't. But they will. Sooner or later they will. And then, I'll put the knife in his heart myself.

He gets up and starts watering the flowers again.

STECCIO

> Keep an eye on Rothstein and these Brooklyn kids. I want the Jews quiet when I make my move.

LUCKY nods and gets up.

STECCIO

> Put that cigarette out inside. Fucks up the flowers.

LUCKY turns and walks away. As he reaches the end of the path, out of STECCIO's view, he throws the cigarette into one of the fountains.

CUT TO

INT. JUDY'S WHOREHOUSE - NIGHT

MEYER and BUGSY are seated across from each other in a booth by the bar. The place is quiet. A few customers and girls flit around in the background. It is raining steadily outside, the drops illuminated by the light of the streetlight outside. MEYER and BUGSY are methodically counting out money. MEYER is putting some of the bills in a separate pile.

BUGSY

> What's that for?

MEYER

> That's for the nestegg.

BUGSY

> The what?

MEYER

> The bank. For a rainy day.

BUGSY

> It's raining now.

They both laugh.

MEYER

> You like 'em to think you're dumb, Benny. But I know better.

MOESY comes up to them from the bar.

MOESY

> There's someone here to see you.

From behind MOESY comes the imposing figure of LUCKY LUCIANO.

LUCKY

> Mind if I sit?

MEYER and BUGSY both looked shocked.

LUCKY

> Thanks.

He pulls up a chair.

LUCKY

> Nasty night out there.

BUGSY recovers his cool first and starts counting bills again.

BUGSY

> So what brings you to Jewtown in weather like this?

LUCKY

> I grew up right near here, you know.

BUGSY

> Oh, yeah?

LUCKY

> Sure, I always had a liken' for the Hebrews. I used to work for this Jew family up on Delancy. I'd go there for the Sabbaths, you know. Light the candles for 'em and all that. Fed me real good. It aint Italian food or nothin', but good stuff.

BUGSY

> That so?

LUCKY

> Sure, I even used to sing them songs sometimes, you know: "*Baruch ata adonai, eloheinu melekh ha-olam...*" That's all I remember.

BUGSY and MEYER look at each other, astounded. Then burst out laughing.

LUCKY

> Hey, I know I aint Kate Smith, but...

BUGSY

> Alright rabbi Luciano, what you want?

LUCKY

> Just wanted to keep the radio tuned in, you know? So you guys don't forget me.

BUGSY

> Well, don't worry about that, fella.

LUCKY

> There's also something you might want to know, fella.

MEYER

> What's that?

BUGSY

Look who's interested all of a sudden.

LUCKY

Steccio is gonna move against Maranzano.

BUGSY stops counting the bills.

MEYER

When?

LUCKY

He doesn't know yet, but he's scared.

MEYER

Nobody wants a war.

LUCKY

He knows that. He also knows if he waits much longer there aint gonna be enough left to bury when Maranzano puts the knife in his back.

MEYER

Can he do it?

LUCKY

Let me put it his way: it's only a matter of time before one of these jokers whacks the other one. This bullshit can't go on much longer.

MEYER

Is Maranzano strong enough?

LUCKY

Not yet, but in another year he will be.

MEYER says nothing, he is deep in thought.

BUGSY

What's your angle, Charlie?

LUCKY

Like I said: you boys aint playin' the same game. I got a lot of guys would love to see both a the Moustache Petes in the East River, but they sure as shit aint gonna raise a hand to make it happen.

MEYER

And you think we will?

LUCKY

I think you're the only ones who can.

BUGSY

Are you crazy? We're gonna whack the two biggest greaseballs in New York? And just so's another buncha greaseballs can take over?

LUCKY

I'm a man of my word. Maranzano and Steccio, they're the both of 'em still livin' in the past. Me and the rest of the boys, though, we want a piece of the future.

BUGSY

And that's us?

MEYER

He's right.

BUGSY

What?

MEYER

There's three hundred thousand Jews in Brooklyn alone. More comin' every day. There's a million Italians walkin' the streets of this city. Divided, fighting each other, we're small time. But together...

LUCKY

Together...

MEYER

Together we could own this city. Together we *are* this city.

BUGSY

Over them two's dead bodies.

MEYER looks at him, but says nothing. There is a pregnant silence.

BUGSY

Rothstein'll never go for it.

LUCKY

Rothstein's no good to any of us. He's a stand up guy, but that's the fact of the matter. He's too scared for his high society rep. Thinks he's a gambler, not a gangster. We gotta start thinkin' like the big shots do. Thinkin' about how far we can go, not how well we can hide.

MEYER

Like a business and not a con.

LUCKY

Yeah.

BUGSY

Shit, I'll shoot both them wop motherfuckers for a dime and a cup of coffee, but I aint doin' it till I know for damn sure what the score is.

MEYER

Benny's right. Now aint the time.

LUCKY

Maybe not, but we got to be ready when it comes, 'cos it won't be long.

He gets up to leave.

MEYER

Where can we reach you?

LUCKY
>You don't. I'll stop by again.

He puts his hat on.

LUCKY
>Keep your eyes open.

He walks out.

MEYER
>Yeah...

BUGSY
>You think he's serious?

MEYER
>Yeah. Yeah, I do.

BUGSY leans in close to MEYER.

BUGSY
>But are we serious? That's the question.

Pause. MEYER looks him right in the eye.

MEYER
>I am.

BUGSY nods.

BUGSY
>So am I.

CUT TO

INT. WAREHOUSE -DAY

Reverse track of ROTHSTEIN walking with BUGSY and MEYER as he inspects one of his booze warehouses. Vats of beer are being hauled out of trucks and stacked against the walls.

ROTHSTEIN
>What do you know about this guy Luciano?

MEYER
>Not much, but he came to us. He's got nothin' to gain and a lot to lose.

ROTHSTEIN
>You think he can bring the Young Turks with him?

MEYER
>He talks like he can.

ROTHSTEIN
> Talk is one thing...

BUGSY
> I got a feelin' about him, boss.

ROTHSTEIN
> A feelin'?

BUGSY
> Yeah, I think he's a stand up guy. He's cold-blooded. I think he can pull it off.

ROTHSTEIN
> Why does he need us, then?

MEYER
> The Italians are all up each other's asses. Everyone knows everybody's business. Everyone talks. Too dangerous. He's got to go outside for help.

ROTHSTEIN
> You think like Benny does?

MEYER
> I think if we don't do somethin' soon we'll be under the thumb of the Italians for another hundred years. This is the best chance we'll ever have.

ROTHSTEIN
> Gimme odds.

MEYER
> Can't do it, boss.

ROTHSTEIN
> 50-50?

MEYER
> 70-30, in our favor.

ROTHSTEIN
> Generous. (He smiles.) You're a hell of a handicapper, little man, but things like this, I like a sure thing. I'm too out in the open. I can't get involved. (Pause.) You boys are on your own with this one. If the shit hits, I gotta turn my back.

MEYER nods.

ROTHSTEIN
> Watch yourselves. These wops are tricky bastards. Look you right in the eyes and smile while they're puttin' the knife in your back. Remember that. (Pause.) And I can tell you this: if you boys are plannin' on startin' a war, I'd find some more boys to do the dirty work. Always keep your own hands clean. Helps the reputation.

BUGSY
> This, from the man that fixed the World Series.

ROTHSTEIN
> They never proved anything.

He smiles and walks away.

CUT TO

INT. NIGHTCLUB BACKROOM - NIGHT

LEPKE leads BUGSY and MEYER out of a noisy nightclub, down a corridor and into a back room. There are waiting five boys, dressed in cheap duds, smoking and looking bored.

LEPKE
>Here's your boys. Meet the Purple Gang.

BUGSY
>The what?

BOY #1
>The Purple Gang.

BUGSY
>What, you all faggots or somethin'?

The BOY snaps open a switchblade.

BOY #1
>Come over here and say that.

MEYER
>That's enough. What are your names?

BOY #1
>Names Abe Reles, everyone calls me Kid Twist. This is Longie Zwillman, Crazy Joe Gold, Eddie Luntz, and that sunk-eyed motherfucker over there is Hyman Finkelstein. We call him the Fink.

BUGSY
>Louie, were'd you find these guys, scrape 'em outta the gutter?

LEPKE
>Simmer down, Benny. These boys are the best. You hear about the hit on Larry Rose? That was them.

BUGSY
>No shit? Did you really have to kill the dog too?

KID TWIST
>I don't like dogs.

BUGSY smiles, then laughs.

BUGSY
>I like this kid.

MEYER
>We got some work for you. Five thousand up front, each, ten at the other end.

The Purple Gang snaps to attention.

KID TWIST
Who you want done?

MEYER
You'll find out when the time comes. If you boys do well, we might consider you for permanent employment. In which case, five thousand is gonna look like pocket change.

KID TWIST
Hell, for a hundred bucks and two Park Avenue whores I'll cut my own mamma in half with a sawed-off shotgun.

BUGSY roars with laughter.

BUGSY
I like this kid!

MEYER
Be ready. We'll be in touch.

MEYER and BUGSY walk out. KID TWIST snaps the blade of his knife back into place.

CUT TO

INT. PARK AVENUE RESTAURANT - NIGHT

MEYER and JENNY are having dinner at a small table against the window. JENNY looks uncomfortable, overwhelmed by the opulent surroundings.

JENNY
Meyer, can you afford this?

MEYER
Don't worry about it.

JENNY
It's just...Meyer, it's so fancy.

MEYER
Long way from Brooklyn, huh?

She smiles.

MEYER
I'm tellin' you, Jenny. I got a good feelin' about some things I'm workin' on.

JENNY
Really?

MEYER
I been workin' this deal for a while...and I think we might have found the right partner. Could be somethin' real big.

JENNY
    Meyer, you know I don't care about money.

MEYER
    Everybody cares about money, Jenny.

JENNY
    What's the deal?

MEYER
    It's a... merger. It's really better for me not to talk about it.

JENNY
    I understand.

MEYER holds up his glass.

MEYER
    To the future.

JENNY
    To the future.

She looks blissfully happy.

                                                            CUT TO

INT. BUGSY'S APARTMENT - NIGHT

We hear the sounds of furious lovemaking, a woman's voice grows louder and louder, approaching climax. Suddenly, there is a furious knocking at the door.

WOMAN'S VOICE
    Don't answer it.

More knocking.

BUGSY'S VOICE
    Aw, shit.

We hear scuffling. Then, a light snaps on. BUGSY, clad in a bathrobe, opens the door. MEYER and JENNY, smiling like teenagers are arm in arm in the foyer.

BUGSY
    This better be good.

MEYER
    Tell him.

JENNY
    We're engaged.

BUGSY
    You're shittin' me!

MEYER shakes his head. BUGSY grabs the both of them in a bear hug.

BUGSY
Mazel tov!

He kisses them both on the cheeks. Behind him a young WOMAN,
clad only in a sheet, appears, looking annoyed.

WOMAN
What's all the excitement?

MEYER and JENNY stare at her for a second. Then all three of them burst into uproarious
laughter.

CUT TO

EXT. MADISON HOTEL - NIGHT

A luxurious auto pulls up in front. The DOORMAN opens the door and ROTHSTEIN gets out.

DOORMAN
Good evening, Mr. Rothstein.

ROTHSTEIN
Good evening, Daniel.

He hands him a substantial tip.

DOORMAN
Thank you, sir.

CUT TO

EXT. PETACCHI'S GENTLEMAN'S CLUB - NIGHT

LUCKY comes out, pulling up the collar of his coat against the cold. We hear music from inside.
He steps to the curb to hail a taxi. A black car pulls up in front of him and several men get out.

MAN #1
How you doin', Lucky?

LUCKY
What's goin' on Gino?

GINO
Same old thing.

LUCKY suddenly realizes that he has been surrounded by the toughs.

GINO
Let's go for a ride, huh?

LUCKY surveys the scene for a moment, realizes there is no escape, and gets in the car.

CUT TO

INT. MADISON HOTEL LOBBY - NIGHT

ROTHSTEIN walks to the front desk, the CLERK smiles as he sees him.

CLERK
>Good evening, Mr. Rothstein, how are you?

ROTHSTEIN
>I'm fine, Claude, thank you.

CLERK
>They're in room 217.

ROTHSTEIN
>Thanks.

CLERK
>What's the game tonight, sir?

ROTHSTEIN
>Gin. Five thousand to start.

CLERK
>Good luck, sir.

ROTHSTEIN tips his hat and goes up the stairs.

CUT TO

INT. CAR - NIGHT

LUCKY is squeezed between two of the goons. He looks uncomfortable, but not panicking.

LUCKY
>So, where we goin'?

GINO
>You'll see when we get there.

LUCKY sighs, looking resigned.

CUT TO

INT. CORRIDOR - NIGHT

ROTHSTEIN walks up to room 217. A young man, clearly a guard, stands next to the door.

ROTHSTEIN
>How you doin' Zig?

ZIG
>Alright. You can go on in. Game's already started.

ROTHSTEIN
>Thanks.

He goes into the room.

>CUT TO

INT. SHACK - NIGHT

LUCKY is tied to a chair in the middle of a one-room tin shack. GINO throws a bucket of water on him. Then another of the toughs punches him in the face.

LUCKY is a mass of bleeding cuts and sores. The beating has been going on for awhile. He coughs up blood, spilling it out on to his shirt. From the shadows behind his tormentors, we hear a voice.

VOICE
>Alright, he's had enough.

From out of the shadows emerges an enormous, broad-shouldered man. He looks slightly grotesque, even monstrous. A scar runs down his cheek and halfway down his neck. He is ALPHONSE MARANZANO.

MARANZANO
>You know who I am?

LUCKY nods.

MARANZANO
>Good. I think it's time we talked a little business.

He pulls up a chair and sits.

MARANZANO
>Jesus, Luciano, you look like shit.

The boys laugh.

LUCKY
>Fuck you, Maranzano.

MARANZANO
>I know you're a little punch-drunk, Lucky, so I'll let that one pass.

LUCKY coughs up blood again.

MARANZANO
>But if you want to get out of here walkin', you'll listen to what I got to say.

LUCKY says nothing.

MARANZANO

Your boss is losin' the game. You know it and I know it. Every day he gets a little weaker and I...I get a little stronger. You're a smart kid, Lucky, you know that. And you know a lotta other smart kids, too. Smart kids like you I could use for these things I gotta do.

Pause.

MARANZANO
No one wants a war, Lucky. War's bad for business, makes enemies, not friends. But things still gotta change, you know? I brought you here 'cause I wanted you to see that I'm a serious man. I mean to do this thing, with you or without you. But if its gotta be, then I'd rather do it with you. What I mean, Lucky, is that, if we play our cards right, there's only one man here that's gotta die. That Sicilian prick boss of yours is goin' down, but that don't mean anybody else got to. You understand what I mean? A little change at the top, that's all. A few small changes down below to make room for my boys here, and everybody's happy. What do think?

LUCKY doesn't answer.

MARANZANO
Well, you don't gotta answer me now. You gotta think it over, work things out in your head.

LUCKY coughs up blood.

MARANZANO
Relax a little. Untie him boys!

They untie him and hold him by the shoulders. He can barely stand on his own.

MARANZANO
Don't take too long. (To his men:) Take him to Mercy General, make sure he gets patched up.

They start to haul him out.

MARANZANO
Be smart, Lucky!

CUT TO

INT. MADISON HOTEL LOBBY - NIGHT

The DESK CLERK is rearranging some flowers near the stairwell. He hears a noise and looks up. His eyes widen with terror.

REVERSE SHOT OF ROTHSTEIN, bleeding horribly from a gunshot wound in his abdomen, careening down the stairs. He gasps, loses his balance, and tumbles down the rest of the way.

CUT TO

INT. HOSPITAL ROOM - DAY

LUCKY, his face bruised and bandaged, slowly opens his eyes. BUGSY and MEYER are sitting by the bed.

LUCKY

> Holy shit. How'd you get in here?

MEYER

> Your boy Frankie.

LUCKY

> He's a good kid.

MEYER

> He'd better be.

LUCKY

> Don't worry about Frankie.

MEYER

> Listen to me, Charlie. Rothstein is dead.

LUCKY

> What?

MEYER

> Bullet in the gut, three o'clock this morning.

LUCKY

> Steccio?

MEYER

> No, some drunk at a high-stakes gin game.

LUCKY laughs.

LUCKY

> Oh, Jesus...who'da thought...

MEYER

> Listen to me, Charlie, Rothstein was the only thing standin' between us and the Petes. With him gone, they are gonna come down on us like a ton of bricks. We got to move now.

LUCKY props himself up in bed.

LUCKY

> That aint all. I had a little meetin' with Maranzano and his boys last night. They want me to throw in with them. They're gonna move against Steccio any day now.

BUGSY

> And when he does, he'll be too strong to take out.

LUCKY

> Can you do it?

MEYER

That aint the question, Charlie. We're out on a fuckin' limb here. We're takin' a big chance. We need to know that if we move you can get the other families to go along. You say yes, and we give the word.

LUCKY looks at them both for a second. Then he nods. MEYER takes a deep breath. BUGSY smiles.

CUT TO

INT. LEPKE'S CLUB - NIGHT

A wall telephone ringing. It rings five or six times before LEPKE picks it up.

LEPKE
Yeah? (Pause) Alright, I'll tell 'em.

He hangs up the phone. We follow him as he opens the door to the backroom. Framed in the doorway are the Purple Gang, smoking and playing cards.

LEPKE
Time to go to work, boys.

CUT TO

INT. SYNAGOGUE - DAY

CLOSE UP of a CANTOR, his eyes closed, intoning a passionate prayer.

REVERSE SHOT of JENNY, in her bridal gown, being walked towards the groom.

It is MEYER and JENNY's wedding. All are assembled, family and friends. BUGSY, DUTCH, LEPKE and MOESY are smartly dressed in the front row.

CUT TO

INT. RESTAURANT - DAY

A large, fashionable Italian place. MARANZANO, wiping his hands with a towel, gets up from his table and shakes the hand of his guest.

REVERSE SHOT of the guest. It is LUCKY LUCIANO.

MARANZANO
Glad you could make it, Salvatore. I knew you was a smart kid.

CUT TO

INT. SYNAGOGUE - DAY

JENNY is circling MEYER. He looks uncomfortable, clad awkwardly in prayer shawl and skullcap. We can hear cooing whispers from the assembled.

CUT TO

EXT. STECCIO'S MANSION -DAY

Two COPS are waiting outside the front door. One of them knocks. A servant opens the door. One of the COPS holds up a piece of paper.

COP #1
> We have a warrant to search the premises.

CUT TO

INT. SYNAGOGUE

MEYER, his head bowed, is reciting a prayer. JENNY looks on, radiant under her veil.

CUT TO

INT. RESTAURANT

MARANZANO is eating furiously, talking at the same time. LUCKY is watching him intently.

MARANZANO
> Times gotta change, you know? You feel good about this, son. Aint no room for bad blood in this thing of ours...

CUT TO

INT. SYNAGOGUE

The CANTOR is singing a passionate prayer before the couple.

CUT TO

INT. STECCIO'S OFFICE -DAY

It is a beautiful mahogany office with a large bay window looking out on his gardens. STECCIO is working, he looks up as his SERVANT leads the COPS in.

SERVANT
> I'm sorry, sir...

COP #1
> Mr. Steccio, we have a warrant to search your office.

STECCIO
> (To the SERVANT) It's alright, Paul, it's alright.

CUT TO

INT. SYNAGOGUE

The CANTOR's prayer reaches a fervent climax.

CUT TO

INT. RESTAURANT

MARANZANO is still talking. LUCKY drains his glass of wine and stands up.

LUCKY
I gotta take a piss.

MARANZANO
I aint stoppin' you.

CUT TO

INT. SYNAGOGUE

The CANTOR, his arms spread, his voice whirling up to one final note.

CUT TO

INT. STECCIO'S OFFICE

The COPS are rummaging around.

STECCIO
Go on, search, you aint gonna find nothin'.

COP #1 turns and STABS STECCIO THROUGH THE HEART, holding his hand over the old man's mouth to muffle his death spasm.

We see the COP's face for the first time, it is KID TWIST RELES.

CUT TO

INT. RESTAURANT

MARANZANO is still eating furiously, waiting for LUCKY to return. The WAITER comes up behind him.

WAITER
More wine, sir?

Without looking back, MARANZANO holds out his glass, the waiter tops it off.

MARANZANO
Thanks.

WAITER
    My pleasure, sir.

THE WAITER SHOOTS MARANZANO THROUGH THE BACK OF THE HEAD, spattering his brains across the perfectly white silk tablecloth. We slowly track upwards until we see that the waiter is LONGIE ZWILLMAN.

                                     CUT TO

INT. SYNAGOGUE

CLOSE UP of the ceremonial glass being wrapped.

                                     CUT TO

INT. STECCIO'S OFFICE

The "COPS" quietly close the door on STECCIO'S body, still in its leather chair, and leave.

                                     CUT TO

INT. SYNAGOGUE

CLOSE UP of the wrapped glass being placed on the floor.

                                     CUT TO

INT. RESTAURANT

LUCKY emerges from the restroom, wiping his hands. LONGIE and him exchange glances, then walk off in opposite directions.

                                     CUT TO

INT. SYNAGOGUE

The assembled wait for the final moment.

                                     CUT TO

INT. STECCIO'S OFFICE

STECCIO in his armchair, the knife protruding from his chest.

                                     CUT TO

INT. RESTAURANT

MARANZANO, face-down on the table.

CUT TO

INT. SYNAGOGUE

MEYER stamps on the glass.

CANTOR
    Mazel Tov!

The audience erupts into cheers, throwing flowers and candy. MEYER and JENNY kiss as man and wife.

CUT TO

INT. DANCE HALL - EVENING

The wedding party is in full flight. People are laughing and drinking and dancing the hora. MEYER and JENNY, looking dazed, are still receiving gifts and congratulations. The boys walk up and hug MEYER.

BUGSY
    I always knew the little man'd be the first to go!

JENNY
    Benny!

BUGSY
    I'm yankin' you, Jen, relax.

JENNY smiles. LEPKE pokes BUGSY's arm and points.

THEIR POV of KID TWIST emerging from the crowd. He says nothing, but nods almost imperceptibly.

REVERSE SHOT of THE BOYS, struck dumb with the magnitude of what has just happened.

Suddenly a dancing circle grabs them and pulls them it. We watch as the room turns into a whirling dervish of dancers holding hands. KID TWIST, his mission accomplished, silently leaves.

CUT TO

INT. BOARDROOM -DAY

Two large doors open and reveal the heads of the New York families seated around a circular boardroom table. LUCKY, MEYER, BUGSY and the rest stride into the room. Behind them comes the Purple Gang.

LUCKY

Good morning gentlemen, I'm sure you've all heard that there's been some changes around here. Me and my associates want to get things clear and out in the open, so there wont be no bad blood over the recent changes in management. Now I'm sure you all know that business is as good as it's ever been. This country loves booze more then they did when it was legal, and every last drop of it gotta come through us. You add in everything that folks like when they drink: gamblin', music, shows, women, and we got ourselves a bona fide industry. We're as big as Henry Ford and we don't even know it. The only difference between us and them is they got a license to steal and we don't. Now, nobody here wants a war. War's bad for business. Draws attention. Stops up the works. Makes everything ten times as hard and fifty times as expensive. It aint worth it to none of us. That's why I called this meetin', so I could do you gentlemen the respect of explaining to your faces how this new arrangement is gonna benefit all of us.

A white-haired OLD DON bangs on the table with his cane.

OLD DON
> What is this shit?! And what the hell are they doin' here? (He points to BUGSY, MEYER and the rest.) You go in with Jews against your own people?!

BUGSY bristles but MEYER shakes his head to tell him to simmer down.

LUCKY
> Aint nobody goin' in against nobody! That's the old country talkin'. This is the new world. We got to stop livin' in the past. Damn near half this city is Jews, whether we like it or not. We can hide from it and stay small, or we can do business. And then...then we can own this city. Gentlemen, what I'm talkin' about is bigger than booze and bigger than gambling and bigger than five dollar whores and crooked crap deals. I'm talkin' about a business. I'm talkin' about organization. I'm talkin' about organized. And a take that we don't count in the thousands; but in the millions. There aint no room for all this old country bullshit about honor and blood. This is America. There's a whole country a suckers out there ripe for the taking and we're too busy fightin' ourselves to take it! What I'm offering you is a city where the Mayor don't brush his teeth without us givin' the ok. I'm offering you an organization where wars get finished here, in this room, instead of out in the streets with machine guns and switchblades. I'm offering you a country where, if you play your cards right, every last one of you will die fat, rich, happy, and with the president of the United States kissin' your ass as they put you in the ground. What I'm offering you, gentlemen, is the future. I suggest you take it.

There is a low murmur from the assembled.

LUCKY
> Meyer?

MEYER shyly takes LUCKY's place at the head of the table.

MEYER
> From now on, this city will be organized like a business corporation. As far as you gentlemen are concerned, Mr. Luciano is Chairman of the Board. Mr. Siegel and I will remain in our independent capacity.

Some of THE DONS look confused.

BUGSY
> That means we don't take orders from nobody.

MEYER

That's right. All of you retain your current territories, plus a piece of what was Steccio and Maranzano's. You'll negotiate the specifics with Mr. Luciano. Any disputes whatsoever between the families will be brought here. Any problems that can't be worked out will be decided by a majority vote. Or, if necessary, by Mr. Luciano, Mr. Siegel, and myself. Any problems that require...drastic solutions, will be handled by our friends, Mr. Reles and his crew.

He indicates the Purple Gang. A BALDING DON speaks up.

BALDING DON
 Are you sayin that if I wanna whack somebody, I gotta have some Jew do it?

He chuckles.

MEYER
 That's right.

LUCKY
 We don't want no more wars gettin' started over some gunsel gettin' whacked. Vendettas are for the old country. These boys can handle it. Steccio and Maranzano'd tell you that, if they was still breathin'.

MEYER
 The remainder of the unclaimed territories go to us. Dutch Schultz will handle booze, and Louie Buchalter will be given the unions.

There is a murmur of discontent. MEYER suddenly becomes very serious, and we begin to sense his authority.

MEYER
 Gentlemen, these conditions are not negotiable.

LUCKY
 I can give you a guarantee, on my honor as a Sicilian, your take will be double what it was last year, and then it'll go up.

There is a whispered consideration among the Dons.

LUCKY
 We need an answer now, my friends. All in favor?

One by one, THE OLD DONS raise their hands.

LUCKY
 Gentlemen, welcome to the new world.

CUT TO

MONTAGE - THE ROARING TWENTIES

Ferocious hot jazz music plays over the following:

INT. BANK - DAY

BUGSY and MEYER walk in toting suitcases.

CUT TO

INT. MANAGER'S OFFICE

The BANK MANAGER, a snappily dressed WASP, opens the suitcases, they are stacked high with hundred dollar bills. He closes them and, smiling, shakes BUGSY's hand.

CUT TO

INT. BOOZE WAREHOUSE - NIGHT

DUTCH and his right hand man, ABADABA BERMAN, a short, balding, bespectacled figure who looks more like an accountant than a gangster, are watching as truck after truck of illegal alcohol is driven into the warehouse. One by one, ABADABA ticks them off on his clipboard.

CUT TO

INT. SPEAKEASY - NIGHT

BUGSY is living it up, surrounded by flappers and admirers. Confetti and steamers cascade down from the ceiling. Behind him, a line of dancing girls are kicking up their heels.

CUT TO

INT. MEYER'S STUDY - NIGHT

MEYER is bent over his work, making notations in a ledger from a small notebook.

CUT TO

EXT. UNION SQUARE PARK - DAY

A massive union demonstration is underway. Hundreds of signs for every union in every profession imaginable. The crowd is shouting and excited, an impassioned speaker whipping them up from the stand.

We PAN DOWN from the stand until we see LEPKE talking intently with some well-dressed men, clearly out of place. They hand him a suitcase surreptitiously, which he passes to MOESY, who is standing behind him. The two men shake hands with LEPKE and disappear uncomfortably into the crowd.

CUT TO

INT. OFFICE WAITING ROOM - DAY

A door opens and a stocky, jolly looking man comes out, slapping LEPKE on the shoulder. He hands LEPKE a cigar and, as LEPKE walks away he bites the end off and spits it in the garbage can. The secretary looks scandalized. The man laughs and goes back into his office. As he closes the door we see that it reads: "OFFICE OF THE HON. JIMMY WALKER, MAYOR OF NEW YORK CITY."

CUT TO

INT. SYNDICATE BOARDROOM - DAY

LUCKY is presiding at the head of the table, surrounded by the assembled heads of the New York families.

LUCKY
    All in favor?

They raise their hands.

CUT TO

EXT. STREET - NIGHT

A man in a long black coat with the collar turned up hurries across the street to a public phone booth. As he dials, a car pulls up alongside. The doors open and BUGSY and KID TWIST lean out toting submachine guns. They open up into the phone booth, turning it into a mass of broken glass and twisted metal. The phone hangs swinging on its cord as the car drives off at full speed.

CUT TO

FAST MONTAGE

- The top of another briefcase full of money slamming down.

- BUGSY dancing the Charleston on a stage surrounded by chorus girls.

- Cascades of trucks pouring into DUTCH's warehouse.

- LEPKE's union boys beating the hell out of a group of scabs.

- LUCKY entering a posh nightclub, the girl at his arm clad in a thick mink coat.

- JENNY, very pregnant, looks in on her husband, he doesn't stir from his work. She turns away, a forlorn look on her face. MEYER, still bent over his work, reaches over and shuts out the light.

The music dissipates into a single, dying note.

CUT TO

INT. SPEAKEASY - NIGHT

An enormous sign reads: "WELCOME 1929". MEYER and BENNY are seated in a secluded corner booth, MEYER with a stack of papers in front of him, he looks concerned and annoyed.

MEYER

You shouldn'ta gone along on the Millman hit, Benny. You're attracting too much attention.

BUGSY

Meyer, you gotta learn to relax, enjoy life. I didn't get into this thing to turn into some banker sittin' in his office all day.

MEYER

It's a question of bein' smart, Benny. You been readin' the papers?

He throws a copy of the morning edition on the table, the headline reads: "DEWEY SWORN IN AS DISTRICT ATTORNEY: PLEDGES WAR AGAINST MOB." Underneath it is a picture of a smiling man in a suit and tie with a small moustache.

BUGSY

Another politician, aint met one who didn't have his price.

MEYER

This guy wants to be president, Benny. That's his price.

BUGSY

So we'll make him president, we made Walker mayor, didn't we?

MEYER

And how long you think that's gonna last? They already got a committee investigation on him. How long you think this country's gonna stay dry? It aint gonna be forever, I can tell you that!

BUGSY

Meyer...

MEYER

Times are changin' Benny, I can feel it. The heats gonna come down on us, and we can't afford to be reckless.

BUGSY

You think I'm reckless, Meyer?

MEYER

I think you like the game too much, Benny. You like bein' the mark, and not the house. You like to throw your change down that hole.

BUGSY

Maybe, little man, maybe. But you know how we got here.

MEYER

I want to do what it takes to stay here, Benny. Watch yourself, alright?

BENNY

Don't worry about me, little man. I can take care of myself.

MEYER lights a cigarette and looks off to the side.

MEYER

That aint what I'm worried about, Benny. This thing is bigger than you. You aint figured that out yet.

We CLOSE IN on the newspaper and the waving figure in the photograph, slowly we...

FADE TO

EXT. CITY HALL - DAY

The man with the moustache, DISTRICT ATTORNEY THOMAS DEWEY, is giving a speech surrounded by reporters and political supporters.

DEWEY
    ...and I furthermore pledge that the scourge of organized crime will no longer be tolerated in New York City!

CUT TO

INT. WAREHOUSE - NIGHT

A squad of police cars burst through the doors, policemen rush out toting tommy guns, the bootleggers throw up their hands.

CUT TO

DEWEY'S SPEECH

DEWEY
    The industries of gambling, bootlegging and prostitution are the shame of this great city and of this great nation!

CUT TO

INT. SPEAKEASY - NIGHT

COPS burst in on the revelers, shoving them up against the wall and throwing bottles of booze shattering on to the floor.

CUT TO

DEWEY'S SPEECH

DEWEY
    I will follow these moguls of vice and iniquity wherever they may seek to hide, even into the hallowed halls of justice themselves!

CUT TO

EXT. STREET - NIGHT

Cops are throwing illegal slot machines into the streets, sending thousands of coins scattering across the asphalt. Reporters are furiously snapping pictures.

                                                                                        CUT TO

DEWEY'S SPEECH

DEWEY
        No one, under my administration, will be allowed to pervert the cause of justice, and
        make vice their profession in this fair city! On that, I pledge my word and my sacred
        honor!

The crowd applauds.

                                                                                        CUT TO

INT. MEYER'S OFFICE - DAY

MEYER is bent over his work, stacks of paper covering his desk. The telephone rings and, without looking up, he picks up the receiver.

MEYER
        I'm working.

He listens for a moment, then puts his hand over his forehead and sighs.

MEYER
        Alright, I'll send somebody down.

                                                                                        CUT TO

INT. COURTHOUSE HALLWAY - DAY

DUTCH is speaking to reporters, flanked by ABADABA BERMAN and his lieutenant, BO WEINBERG, a stocky bear of a man in a long coat.

REPORTER
        Mr. Schultz, how do you react to the charges District Attorney Dewey is making that
        you are, in fact, the boss of the entire bootlegging industry on the Lower East Side?

DUTCH
        Well, if that's his charge, why don't he charge me with it?

The REPORTERS laugh.

DUTCH
        Tax evasion? What's this tax evasion? Let me tell you, you should see what I sent the
        feds last year. They oughta go lookin' for the real thieves up in Washington.

More laughter.

REPORTER

    Mr. Schultz, what do you think of Mr. Dewey?

DUTCH

    Let me tell you something, this is an ambitious man. Now, I got no problem with ambition. I'm an ambitious man myself. But I never persecuted an honest man to get ahead, never. That's the difference between me and him.

He waves to reporters and begins to exit amidst the flashing of flashbulbs.

REPORTER

    Are you worried, Mr. Schultz?

DUTCH

    Worried? I don't worry 'bout nothin'.

                                          CUT TO

INT. MEYER'S OFFICE - NIGHT

DUTCH, ABADABA, and BO WEINBERG are seated across from LEPKE, MOESY, LUCKY, BUGSY and MEYER. DUTCH is pacing the floor, furiously agitated.

DUTCH

    Tax evasion! He's gonna send me up for tax evasion! I'm gonna cut this motherfucker into pieces and throw him in the East River! I'll skin the prick alive and make him dance while I'm doing it!

LUCKY

    Calm down, Dutch.

DUTCH

    Don't tell me to calm down, you Sicilian prick! You aint lookin' at ten years in Dannamora! Look what they gave Capone!

MEYER

    It aint gonna help gettin' hysterical about it.

DUTCH

    Hysterical?!

BUGSY

    Sit down, Dutch.

DUTCH takes a deep breath and sits down.

DUTCH

    All I wanna know is what we're gonna do about this cocksucker Dewey.

BUGSY

    We don't even know if he's got a case.

DUTCH

    Abadaba?

ABADABA

In my opinion, it's unlikely that Dewey would undertake such a high profile case without, at least, a very good chance of conviction.

DUTCH

You got that?

BUGSY

So buy him.

ABADABA

Already attempted.

LUCKY

This guy's a crusader.

DUTCH

That's right. It's me or him, and I'm gonna do what I gotta do, whether you boys like it or not. It aint your heads in the noose.

LUCKY

What you got in mind?

DUTCH says nothing.

LUCKY

No way.

DUTCH

I...

MEYER

Dutch, this guy is the District Attorney of New York City. Do you have any idea what kind of heat would come down on us?

DUTCH

Worried about your skin, Meyer? I'm worried about mine.

MEYER

It's out of the question.

DUTCH

My guy don't think so. Bo?

BO

Dewey's a boy scout. No booze, no dames, no games of chance. Every day he leaves his apartment at nine thirty and walks to the corner drugstore, where he buys the morning paper and a bottle of milk. No bodyguards.

MEYER

No fucking way.

BO

We can get to him, Meyer. We can get to anybody.

MEYER

    It aint a question of gettin' to him.

DUTCH

    What the fuck is this? Is Bo Weinberg the only kike I can trust in this town?

MEYER

    Calm down, Dutch.

DUTCH

    I aim to do this thing, Meyer. I aint lettin this goyishe shmuck put me away.

LUCKY

    Dutch, this is a bigger thing than you. You do this and it's on all of us.

DUTCH

    We've been through a lot, boys. You're like brother's to me. But I wont play the fall guy. If this fuck comes after me, I'll have his body in the East River and his head for my fuckin' wall. Let's go boys.

He gets up to leave, his boys follow him.

LUCKY

    Dutch. Be smart.

DUTCH

    I always am, Charlie.

He leaves. There is a long silence. The men look at the floor, their heads bowed.

LUCKY

    Gentlemen?

One by one, each of them nods their heads.

LUCKY

    Take care of it, Benny.

                                CUT TO

INT. MEYER'S APARTMENT - NIGHT

A weary MEYER opens the door and comes in, hanging his hat up on the stand and putting his briefcase on a chair. He looks haggard, exhausted. JENNY appears in the doorway to the kitchen, in her nightgown.

MEYER

    Hi, Jen.

JENNY

    The kids went to sleep hours ago.

MEYER

    Yeah, I got held up at the office.

He takes off his coat and goes towards his study.

JENNY
      The police were here today.

He looks indifferent.

MEYER
      Yeah? You call the lawyer?

JENNY
      They went through the children's things.

MEYER
      Yeah, it's just harassment, Jenny. I told you about this.

JENNY
      Meyer, what's happening?

MEYER
      Nothing.

He goes into his study and places some papers on the desk. JENNY stands behind him in the doorway.

JENNY
      Meyer...

MEYER
      Jenny, I got work to do.

He starts scribbling.

JENNY
      Do you think I'm stupid, Meyer?

MEYER looks up at her, surprised.

MEYER
      What?

JENNY
      You think I don't know what's going on? You think I don't read the papers?

MEYER stands up and draws close to her, she backs away a bit.

MEYER
      Jenny, whatever you read in the papers...

JENNY
      I grew up with you, Meyer! I'm from those streets too! You think I don't know what Benny is? What Dutch is? What Louie is?

MEYER
      What? What are we?

Tears begin to fall from Jenny's eyes.

JENNY
How many men have you killed, Meyer?

MEYER's eyes suddenly become cold and dark, like BUGSY's eyes at the moment of murder.

MEYER
Me? I never killed nobody.

He turns and goes back into his study, slamming the door in JENNY's face.

CUT TO

INT. OPIUM DEN - NIGHT

The door opens, and we see BUGSY, framed in shadow, as he slowly steps inside. A Chinese waiter comes up to him but BUGSY waves him away. Gingerly, he steps between the prostrate bodies of the smokers, some of whom are sleeping, others staring trancelike into space. He approaches the far corner of the room, where we see BO WEINBERG lying on a bunk, smoking a long pipe. BO puts the pipe down and turns on to his back. He opens his eyes.

BO'S POV looking up at BUGSY from a low angle.

BO
Hey, Benny. What are you doin' here?

BUGSY
Tried to call you, nobody answered, so I figured you'd be here.

BO
Yeah...How long I been sleepin'?

BUGSY
Couldn't tell you, Bo.

BO
You want a smoke?

BUGSY
No, I aint got enough brains as it is.

BO smiles.

BO
(Dreamily.) You aint sore at me, are you Benny?

BUGSY
No. I aint sore at you, Bo.

BO
That's good. There aint no room for hard feelings between friends.

BUGSY
Yeah. Yeah, I guess that's true.

BO
        Oh, Benny, I had the most beautiful dream...

He closes his eyes and smiles. BUGSY smiles back. Then he takes a silenced automatic from under his jacket and FIRES THREE TIMES into BO. BO gasps, then exhales violently and goes limp on the bunk.

BUGSY puts his gun away and looks around. The waiter catches his eye, then disappears into the shadows. BUGSY pulls his jacket around him and walks out, leaving BO bleeding into the white sheets lit with yellow from the dim lamps above.

                                           CUT TO

INT. DUTCH'S BAR - NIGHT

DUTCH is playing cards with ABADABA BERMAN and some of his boys. The place is shuttered and dark, a driving thunderstorm is pouring down rain outside. A lightening flash and thunder illuminate the scene for a brief moment. A radio is softly playing "Bye Bye Blackbird."

HENCHMAN
        Pissin' down out there aint it?

DUTCH
        Where the hell is Bo?

ABADADA
        Relax, Arthur, he's probably doped up at the Chinks again.

DUTCH
        Fuckin' hophead. Third time in two weeks he's gone on the pipe. When's Dewey's tail
        gonna call?

ABADABA
        Won't be long. You know, you're gonna have to lam it for awhile after this goes down.

DUTCH
        Do me a favor, Bernie, don't help me, alright?

ABADABA looks exasperated, but says nothing.

                                             CUT TO

EXT. BAR - NIGHT

We PAN SLOWLY along the rain soaked window, watching the players inside.

                                           CUT TO

INT. DUTCH'S BAR - NIGHT

DUTCH throws down his cards and gets up.

DUTCH
I'm gonna take a piss. Call me if you hear anything.

ABADABA
Alright, Arthur.

DUTCH goes to the bathroom. His boys start dealing the next round.

The bar door SILENTLY OPENS. We see only the shoes of the four men who enter out of the driving rain. The song rises in intensity and volume.

CUT TO

INT. BATHROOM

DUTCH zips up his pants and starts fastidiously washing his hands.

CUT TO

INT. DUTCH'S BAR

In TOTAL SILENCE, except for the lilting music, ABADABA and the HENCHMEN ARE GUNNED DOWN IN A HAIL OF MACHINE GUN BULLETS.

CUT TO

INT. BATHROOM

CLOSE UP of DUTCH'S FACE. He looks into the mirror as he hears the shots. He knows what is coming.

CUT TO

INT. DUTCH'S BAR

We see the legs of the assassins as they walk past the bodies towards the bathroom.

CUT TO

INT. BATHROOM

CLOSE UP of DUTCH. He slowly wipes the water away from his face. We CLOSE IN on his almost emotionless eyes.

The door BURSTS OPEN and BUGSY, flanked by KID TWIST RELES and two other men toting tommy guns, comes in, his pistol hanging at his side.

DUTCH just looks at him, a look of silent, despairing recognition on his face, a bath towel clasped between his hands. He spreads his arms, as if in an act of supplication or acceptance.

BUGSY raises his pistol and FIRES FIVE SHOTS into DUTCH's chest. They echo like thunderclaps around the empty bathroom. DUTCH pitches backwards into the white tile wall and slides down into a heap on the floor. BUGSY pockets his gun and leads his men out.

CUT TO

INT. DUTCH'S BAR

BUGSY and his boys walk calmly past the carnage and out into the driving storm.

CUT TO

INT. BATHROOM

OVERHEAD SHOT of DUTCH'S BODY. He is murmuring to himself in a barely audible whisper. We RISE SLOWLY UPWARDS and...

FADE TO

INT. HOSPITAL ROOM - NIGHT

DUTCH in lying in a hospital bed, still whispering to himself, as a stenographer taps away, recording every word.

CUT TO

INT. MEYER'S OFFICE - DAY

BUGSY is holding the morning paper, which reads: "MOBSTER DUTCH SCHULTZ DIES AFTER THREE DAY COMA".

BUGSY
>Says he babbled for three days and didn't give 'em nothin but gibberish.

MEYER
>He always looked out for his friends.

There is a mournful silence between them.

MEYER
>Read page three, the vote on Prohibition is on Thursday.

BUGSY
>So what do we do on Friday?

MEYER
>Start lookin' for work.

BUGSY
>C'mon, Meyer. The unions and the slots'll keep us in business.

MEYER

    I don't know, Benny. This country's changing. Maybe we'd be better off lookin' for greener pastures. I been checkin' out a few options offshore.

BUGSY

    Meyer, are you crazy?

MEYER

    Benny, we just took out the life's work of a DA who thinks he's gonna be president in four years, eight at the most. I don't know what he's gonna do, but we aint gonna like it.

                                    CUT TO

INT. OFFICE - DAY

The doors open and we see LUCKY seated at his desk, a SECRETARY leaning over him. A COP shows his badge.

COP

    Are you Salvatore Luciano?

                                      CUT TO

INT. BAR - NIGHT

MOESY SEDWAY, KID TWIST, and LONGIE ZWILLMAN are playing cards in the back room suddenly the doors burst open and a dozen feds toting tommy guns lunge in.

                                      CUT TO

INT. OFFICE - DAY

The COPS are putting the cuffs on LUCKY as his secretary looks helplessly on.

COP

    You are under arrest for engaging in illegal management of a house of prostitution.

LUCKY laughs uproariously.

LUCKY

    You gotta be kidding me! (To his SECRETARY) Honey, call the little man.

                                      CUT TO

INT. BAR - NIGHT

LONGIE ZWILLMAN goes for his gun and is MOWED DOWN where he stands. KID TWIST and MOESY don't move, their hands in the air.

                                      CUT TO

INT. PRISON VISITING ROOM - DAY

BUGSY and MEYER are huddled in front of the bars, talking to LUCKY, who looks ludicrous in his prison blues.

LUCKY

> Jesus fucking Christ, do you believe this? The one thing I didn't do and this is what they hang me with.

MEYER

> It don't look good, Charlie. Dewey wants blood. The word's down from the top, some say Roosevelt himself.

LUCKY

> That no-legged son of a bitch.

BUGSY

> All the witnesses are under lock and key. They got Kid Twist and Moesy. Looks like Kid Twist is singing big time. They got him holed up at the Madison, twenty-four hour guard.

LUCKY

> Can you get around it?

BUGSY

> I'm workin' on it.

MEYER

> Lucky, we gotta think of ourselves here, we got a lot of light on us. If we don't get a license for our dogs Dewey'll put us away for eight to ten.

LUCKY sighs angrily.

LUCKY

> How about Moesy?

MEYER

> Looks like we can get bail, sympathetic judge.

LUCKY

> How much did his sympathies run us?

MEYER

> You don't wanna know.

LUCKY

> You think he told 'em anything?

BUGSY

> Moesy's solid. C'mon, he was with us from the beginning; from before the beginning.

LUCKY

> We're all solid, Benny, till they get those lights on you and start talkin' about twenty five to life.

MEYER

Lucky, we don't think he gave 'em anything.

LUCKY

You wanna take that chance?

BUGSY

As long as he's in jail we can't touch him anyways.

LUCKY

So get him out of jail.

There is a long pause.

LUCKY

Think of yourselves, boys. You're the ones in trouble now. Me? Every day I know exactly where I stand.

CUT TO

EXT. COURTHOUSE - DAY

MOESY is being led out of the doors by BUGSY and some of his boys. Reporters crowd around.

BUGSY

Sorry, boys, he aint got nothin' to say!

He pushes MOESY into a waiting car, than turns to the reporters.

BUGSY

Here's your picture, boys!

He doffs his hat and the flashbulbs go off.

CUT TO

INT. BAR - NIGHT

It is a fashionable looking speakeasy, completely empty but for a forlorn looking bartender.

BUGSY

How's it goin' Joe?

JOE

What can I tell you, Benny? Repeal's killin' me. The good times are over.

BUGSY

Moe, siddown, I'll buy you a drink, celebrate.

MOESY

Sure Benny, let me take a piss first.

BUGSY laughs.

BUGSY

    Alright, you earned it.

MOESY goes into the bathroom. BUGSY leans against the bar, looking at his fingernails.

BUGSY

    Joe, take a walk.

JOE

    Aw, Jeez, Benny, not here...

BUGSY

    Take a walk.

JOE grabs his coat and hurries out the door. BUGSY looks at his watch, then takes a silenced .45 out of his belt and pumps a round into the breach. He looks at his watch again, then goes to the bathroom door and opens it.

                                                     CUT TO

INT. BATHROOM

BUGSY steps inside, his gun held just behind his back.

BUGSY

    Hey Moesy, you fall in?

He opens the door all the way and sees that the room is empty; the back window is open and hanging loose on its hinges. BUGSY dashes to the window and clambers through it.

                                                     CUT TO

EXT. ALLEY - DAY

BUGSY lands on his feet like a cat. He looks left and right, coiled for attack. He sees nothing. There is no trace of MOESY SEDWAY. BUGSY pockets his gun and sighs.

BUGSY

    Ah shit...

                                                     CUT TO

INT. COURTHOUSE - DAY

LEPKE, MEYER, BUGSY, and LUCKY are huddled in a corner outside the courtroom. They speak in whispers.

LUCKY

    You lost him?

BUGSY

    Don't start.

LUCKY

How do you lose a six foot Jew with a mug like Moesy's?

BUGSY

Shut the fuck up, Charlie.

LUCKY

You listen to me, Benny. I've always respected you, but this is my life here.

MEYER

It don't matter, Charlie. Wherever he's gone, Moesy aint showin' his face to nobody, not to us and not to the feds.

LEPKE

So that leaves 'em with Kid Twist.

MEYER

And whatever Moesy told 'em, and from what I'm hearing, it was plenty.

BUGSY

But it don't mean shit if they aint got Kid Twist in court to back it up.

MEYER

Maybe yes and maybe no, but the Kid Twist problem has gotta be take care of.

LUCKY

Listen to the little man, Benny.

BUGSY

Don't worry about Twist, it's in the works.

LUCKY

It'd better be. Ten years is enough for an old timer like me. What Twist knows...

LEPKE

...could mean the chair for all of us.

There is a long pause.

BUGSY

I'll take care of it.

An expensively dressed LAWYER comes out of the courtroom.

LAWYER

Mr. Luciano, they're back.

CUT TO

INT. COURTROOM - DAY

The JUDGE is speaking, as the courtroom and the boys look on.

JUDGE

Salvatore Luciano, having been found guilty of the crime of conspiring to violate the laws of the State of New York regarding vice and prostitution, including conspiracy with person or persons unknown to violate said laws, I hereby sentence you to no less than ten and no more than twelve years in the state penitentiary. Court is adjourned.

He bangs his gavel.

CUT TO

INT. NIGHTCLUB - NIGHT

LEPKE, BUGSY, MEYER, and LUCKY are celebrating, drinking glasses of champagne as a noisy party goes on behind them.

LUCKY

We have a saying in Italian: go where fate takes you, or it drags you there by the heels. Gentlemen, to the new era.

They drink.

LUCKY

I'm putting a lot of faith in you boys, don't let me down.

BUGSY

Hey, we'll be seein' you every week. You're still chairman of the board of wops, ya know.

They laugh.

MEYER

Good luck, Charlie, we'll take care of everything.

LUCKY

It's a new world, boys. Booze is dead as my grandmother, God rest. It's all gonna be in the numbers now, slots, games, horses, dogs, even. That's the future.

BUGSY

Don't forget about Louie's workin' men.

LEPKE

My boys print money.

LUCKY

Sooner or later, they'll clean us out of that too, but the numbers...Even with a depression on, a man'll never shake his belief that fate'll be kind to him. Poor bastards. Aint that right, Meyer?

MEYER

Why rob a bank when they'll come and give you the money, and pay for the privilege?

LUCKY

That's right. All we need is a place where our...talents are truly appreciated, and a whole nation of suckers'll be lining up to throw their money down the hole.

BUGSY

With us at the bottom?

They all laugh again.

LUCKY

Watch yourselves, boys. It's gonna be some hard times coming.

BUGSY

Aint nothin' harder than us, Salvatore.

LUCKY

To the future.

They clink glasses and drink.

LUCKY

Salut paisanos.

BUGSY

L'chaim.

LUCKY puts down his glass, dons on his coat, and walks over to the door, where two uniformed cops are waiting.

LUCKY

OK, let's go.

The boys watch through the window as the cops put LUCKY in a police car and drive away.

CUT TO

INT. HOTEL HALLWAY - NIGHT

A lone policeman is seated in a chair outside one of the rooms, looking bored and sleepy. We see several figures approach him, but we cannot see their faces. One of them turns and hands him a wad of bills. We see that it is BUGSY. The cop nods and pockets the bills. The men open the door and go inside. We PULL BACK SLOWLY as the cop slowly counts the bills in silence. After a few moments, the door opens and BUGSY comes out, followed by his boys. They disappear down the hallway.

The cop watches them go, then gingerly opens the door as we...

CUT TO

INT. HOTEL ROOM - NIGHT

The room is a mess, the bed overturned, the furniture broken up and destroyed. The side window is smashed and the curtains billow in the night breeze. The cop carefully steps through the wreckage and looks out the window.

We SWING OVER AND DOWN to see KID TWIST RELES's body smashed on the pavement five stories below.

CUT TO

INT. PRISON VISITING ROOM - DAY

LEPKE, BUGSY, and MEYER are seated across from LUCKY, in prison clothes again, as he reads a newspaper whose headline reads: WITNESS RACKETEER JUMPS TO HIS DEATH.

LUCKY
Looks like it aint only stockbrokers jumpin' outta windows these days.

BUGSY
Yeah, he smashed the hell out of his room and jumped. Musta gone nuts.

LUCKY
Yeah, he beat his own head in too before he did it.

BUGSY
Twist was a tough kid.

LUCKY
Benny, I don't know what we'd do without you.

LEPKE
We got more problems.

LUCKY
Imagine my surprise.

LEPKE
Dewey's pokin' around my union guys, and not just the stitchers and the truck drivers; the big boys, pension funds, health funds, mayor's liaison...

LUCKY
What's he got?

MEYER
So far, nothing. But if he don't get somethin' soon, he's gonna start writing his own tune.

LUCKY
What do you wanna do?

They look over at BUGSY.

BUGSY
Gotta wait on this one, boys.

LEPKE
How long you want me to wait Meyer? Till they got me hooked into the chair?

BUGSY
What do you want me to do, Louie? I can't kill 'em all.

LEPKE
If you can't, I will.

CLOSE UP of LEPKE's face. We HOLD for a long moment, as he stares at BUGSY in silence.

CUT TO

MONTAGE - THE CRACKDOWN

Over a slow, paintive piano and trumpet ballad, like a lament from a New Orleans funeral.

- COPS burst into a hotel room, where we see three UNION MEN and a PROSTITUTE shot to pieces by machine guns.

- A photograph of a UNION DELEGATE shot through the head, lying dead in the street, surrounded by onlookers.

- A crime scene being photographed, a man lies in his office chair, his throat cut. Above his head is a plaque reading: "FROM THE GRATEFUL MEMBERS OF GARMENT WORKERS 1177".

- A UNION DELEGATE hanging from the rafters of a garment warehouse, the cops are cutting him down.

- A newspaper reading "UNION HALL BURNS TO THE GROUND, ARSON SUSPECTED, 13 DIE," over a photograph of a burning building.
129.

- A man lying dead in an alleyway in a pool of blood. The image slowly fades to grainy black and white, and we PULL OUT to REVEAL:

INT. MEYER'S OFFICE - NIGHT

MEYER and BUGSY are seated crosswise in easy chairs in MEYER's darkly lit office. MEYER is looking at the picture we have just seen in the newspaper, the headline over it reads: "UNION BLOODBATH CONTINUES, TOP PENSION FUND ADMINISTRATOR SLAIN."

MEYER
    Benny, I think this is the first time we got trouble you didn't have nothin' to do with.

BUGSY
    He's just scared, little man. I gotta hand it to Lepkele, I knew he was tough, but this is fuckin' impressive.

MEYER
    He's killing us, Benny. Union payoffs have dropped to nothing. He's wiping everybody out, friends and enemies.

BUGSY
    Maybe Dutch was right, we shoulda killed Dewey when he was still small time.

MEYER
    If it wasn't Dewey, it'd be somebody else. This is bigger than any of us.

BUGSY
    Aint nothin' bigger than us, Meyer. Remember that.

MEYER
> You got delusions of grandeur, Benny. That's what makes you beautiful.

BUGSY
> (Smiling.) Shut the fuck up, little man.

MEYER looks at his watch.

MEYER
> We gotta go. Lepkele's got a surprise for us.

BUGSY gets up sleepily from his chair.

BUGSY
> I can't wait.

> CUT TO

INT. MADISON SQAURE GARDEN - NIGHT

OVERHEAD SHOT of a massive pro-German Bund rally. The assembled mass are clad in black shirts and Nazi-style uniforms. On the stage, a speaker is doing his best Hitler imitation.

SPEAKER
> ...And we will no longer permit the lesser races, the Jew and his nigger hordes and the Catholics and their king in Rome hurl this country into another pointless war against the great German nation and the great German people!

The crowd roars with approval, giving the Nazi salute.

We PAN UPWARDS into the upper rafters of the stadium, where we find LEPKE, BUGSY and MEYER watching the proceedings. BUGSY turns to LEPKE.

BUGSY
> The things you see when you don't have enough guns. How much longer are we gonna have to listen to this?

LEPKE looks at his watch.

LEPKE
> About another minute.

Suddenly, from the back of the hall, a mass of union toughs pour into the stadium, toting crowbars, bats and signs reading "DEATH TO FASCISM," "TO HELL WITH HITLER," and "SUPPORT THE POPULAR FRONT." Before the stunned Nazis can react, THE UNION MEN START BEATING THE LIVING SHIT OUT OF THEM.

LEPKE
> They got here early.

They turn and disappear into the shadows.

> CUT TO

EXT. MADISON SQUARE GARDEN - NIGHT

BUGSY and MEYER are walking away from the carnage. Behind them, the Nazis are being hurled into the street and beaten by LEPKE's union men.

Out of the crowd, a figure emerges, waving to them, it is FRANK COSTELLO.

BUGSY
What's up Frank? How's the luck of the Irish?

COSTELLO
Still holdin' out. Lucky needs to see you.

MEYER
What? In Dannemora? When?

COSTELLO
Tomorrow. Says he's got an important meeting.

MEYER
With who?

CUT TO

INT. WARDEN'S OFFICE - DAY

BUGSY and MEYER are seated next to LUCKY, who is wearing prison clothes. Before them are seated two men in starched suits and ties. One of them is a silent figure wearing a federal badge. The other we recognize. It is THOMAS DEWEY.

DEWEY
Mr. Lansky, Mr. Siegel, I'm sure you know who I am, even though we've never had the pleasure of meeting personally.

MEYER
We know who you are.

BUGSY
You been causin' us a lot of trouble the last few years, boy scout.

DEWEY
I hope that, as a result of this meeting, we can put our differences behind us.

BUGSY
What is this, a courtesy call from the hangman?

MEYER
Shut up, Benny. Let him talk.

DEWEY
I'm glad to see that one of you is of a sensible mindset. I think that some common sense on both our parts may result in our considerable mutual benefit.

MEYER

What are you sellin'?

DEWEY

The situation is simply this: As you gentlemen may be aware, it is the opinion of many in this country that war with Germany and Japan is inevitable.

BUGSY

About time you started dealin' with that goose-stepping prick.

MEYER

Benny...

DEWEY

The federal government... (He nods towards the silent figure next to him.) ...is very concerned with possible German infiltration and sabotage in this city, especially given the volatile international situation.

MEYER

Of course.

DEWEY

It is their belief that the Manhattan docks and, particularly, the dockworkers are especially vulnerable to such subversion.

BUGSY

What's this got to do with us?

MEYER

Let him talk, Benny.

DEWEY

As you know, many of the dockworkers are Italian Americans, most of them recent immigrants.

LUCKY

Those boys are as patriotic as any Kansas farmboy you can find, and change.

DEWEY

I'm sure that's the case, Mr. Luciano. Nonetheless, it would be disturbingly easy for the Italian fascist government and their German allies to place agents among the Italian dockworkers. So far, our efforts to combat such infiltration have been... ineffective.

LUCKY

You don't say.

DEWEY

Therefore, the federal government... and myself... are prepared to make certain concessions to Mr. Luciano in exchange for his... assistance on this problem.

MEYER

What kind of concessions?

DEWEY

Mr. Luciano's sentence will be commuted and he will be released on condition that he be deported to the nation of which he is a citizen, namely, Italy, and that he never return to the United States. Considering the length of Mr. Luciano's sentence and the unlikelihood of his parole, I think this offer is most generous.

BUGSY

Again, what does this have to do with us?

DEWEY

Mr. Luciano has requested certain further concessions on our part, therefore we are also prepared... or, rather, I am prepared... to offer a cessation of our efforts to prosecute both yourself and Mr. Lansky.

MEYER

But it don't come free, does it?

DEWEY

No, it doesn't. I'm afraid that we require... a scapegoat.

BUGSY

Scapegoat?

DEWEY

A sacrificial lamb.

MEYER

Who?

DEWEY

Louis Bouchalter.

MEYER

No.

DEWEY

Mr. Lansky, Mr. Bouchalter's prosecution is inevitable. It could not be stopped without the obvious indication of impropriety on our part. Furthermore, I am well aware of the price incurred by Mr. Bouchalter's recklessness in recent weeks. Your union organization is collapsing.

CUT TO

INT. PRISON CELL - NIGHT

LEPKE is sitting on the bunk in prison blues. The door opens and two policemen lead him out, holding him by the elbows.

CUT TO

INT. WARDEN'S OFFICE

DEWEY continues.

DEWEY

My interests demand that Louis Bouchalter face justice for his crimes.

CUT TO

INT. PRISON HALLWAY

LEPKE being lead down the hallway; his face impassive as stone.

CUT TO

INT. WARDEN'S OFFICE

DEWEY
      Your interests demand that Mr. Bouchalter's union rampage be brought to an end, and that further efforts to harass your organization cease.

CUT TO

INT. THE DEATH ROOM - NIGHT

CLOSE UP of LEPKE'S hands being strapped down.

CLOSE UP of the electrode being lowered on to his head.

CUT TO

INT. WARDEN'S OFFICE

DEWEY
      I'm sure that you gentlemen can see how this arrangement is of mutual benefit to us all.

CUT TO

INT. THE DEATH ROOM

CLOSE UP of the switch being thrown.

CUT TO

INT. PRISON HALLWAY

The lights go dim for a moment.

CUT TO

INT. WARDEN'S OFFICE

THREE SHOT of BUGSY, LUCKY, and MEYER looking stoically at the floor. DEWEY and the FEDERAL AGENT stand up.

DEWEY

I'm glad we could reach an agreement here today. I'm sure you can see that reconciliation is in all our best interests.

He heads for the door. As he leaves, the FEDERAL AGENT turns back.

FED

Gentlemen, this conversation never occurred.

The three friends do not answer.

CUT TO

INT. MEYER'S APARTMENT - NIGHT

MEYER comes in, looking even more fatigued than the last time. He places his briefcase on the chair and takes off his coat and hat. Slowly, he shuffles into the kitchen and starts making himself a sandwich. Behind him, we see that JENNY is standing in the doorway, slightly out of focus.

JENNY

You gave him up, didn't you?

MEYER

I don't know what you're talking about, Jen.

She holds up a newspaper which reads: "UNION RACKETEER LEPKE DIES IN THE CHAIR."

JENNY

You gave him up, didn't you?

MEYER

Jenny...

JENNY

He was your friend. Wasn't he?

MEYER

He was my friend.

JENNY

Why?

He starts to push past her, but she erupts in rage and starts pounding her fists into his chest.

JENNY

Talk to me! Talk to me you son of a bitch!

MEYER

Stop it Jenny! You're hysterical!

JENNY

He was just a boy! Just a boy you grew up with! You knew him when he was just a boy!

MEYER

What do you want from me?

JENNY

I want you to stop lying! I want you to stop playing me like you play everybody else!

He turns and starts down the hallway, but she follows after him.

JENNY

You think I don't know where the money comes from? How long Meyer? How long do you think God will watch us live on blood money?

Suddenly, MEYER turns to face her. For the first time, there is rage in his eyes.

MEYER

God! What do you know about God? What do you know about blood money? It's all blood money, Jenny! You think Roosevelt made his money by the sweat of his hands? How many had to bleed to make him president?

JENNY

Stop it, Meyer!

MEYER

What do you want from me? You want to go back to Delancy Street? Look where we are! I gave you all of this! I gave you the car! I gave you the money! I gave you your life!

JENNY

Stop it, Meyer! Stop it!

MEYER

We live in a world of thieves, Jenny. And I'm the only honest man alive.

JENNY

How much did they give you for Lepkele? How much was he worth?

MEYER

I don't know what you're talking about, Jenny. I don't know what you're talking about.

He goes into his study and slams the door.

CUT TO

INT. LUCKY'S HOTEL ROOM -NIGHT

A wild farewell party is in progress, people are covered in streamers and confetti. BUGSY, MEYER, and LUCKY are seated in the center of the room, drinking champagne. BUGSY and LUCKY have girls on their laps.

LUCKY

Won't be so bad to see the old country. This place don't seem so friendly no more.

MEYER

You're right, Lucky. The future's overseas.

BUGSY

I gotta hand it to you, Charlie, you was the best Jew the wops ever made.

LUCKY

    I'll drink to that.

He downs his champagne.

MEYER

    We all got some changes coming on.

LUCKY

    Remember what I told you boys: by the heels.

MEYER

    I've already started relocating some of our interests to Cuba and the West Coast.

BUGSY

    The little man's got a hard on for Havana.

MEYER

    A businessman's paradise, my friends: the future.

LUCKY

    (Gesturing towards BUGSY) You tell him yet?

BUGSY

    Tell me what?

MEYER looks down into his drink.

MEYER

    You're relocating, Benny.

BUGSY

    I'm what?

MEYER

    Me and Lucky, we...

LUCKY

    We need your expertise elsewhere, Benny. New York is a closed shop, too many people know our names, too many people know our game; it's time to spread our wings.

BUGSY

    What the fuck are you talking about?

MEYER

    We're sending you to LA.

BUGSY

    To LA?

LUCKY

    On a trial basis, let's say.

BUGSY

    You pushin' me out, little man?

MEYER

It aint like that, Benny.

LUCKY

Benny, listen. There aint nothin' out there in LA, its open ground, ready for the fruits of industry. All they got out there is the Farina mob, and that aint nothing but a coupla washed up Italians makin' dimes and nickels on the wire. We need somebody serious out there, Benny, someone to take the joint by the balls.

MEYER

Truth is, Benny, you been havin' your own way for too long. There's too many New York stiffs with your fingerprints on 'em. Out here, it's only a matter of time.

BUGSY

So it's for my own good.

LUCKY

For your good and our good, Benny. For the good of all of us.

BUGSY looks unconvinced.

LUCKY

Come on, Benny. Sun, movie stars, Hollywood, palm trees, plenty of starvin' actresses to fuck. It's a new world.

BUGSY smiles a half-smile.

BUGSY

I always did hate the weather up here.

LUCKY

To the new world.

He raises his glass.

ALL

To the new world!

CUT TO

EXT. DOCKS - NIGHT

LUCKY and MEYER are standing at the gangplank of a large ocean liner, shaking hands.

MEYER

Salut, paisan.

LUCKY

Zaigazunt, little man.

LUCKY kisses him on both cheeks.

LUCKY

We conquered the world, little man. Now the world's conquering us.

MEYER

Just a change of venue, Lucky. You said it yourself.

LUCKY

Yeah... Aint gonna be the same though, Meyer. The time for punks and shitkickers is over. When this war is done its gonna be a businessman's world, dollars and cents, not guns and muscle... Your boy Benny don't understand that.

MEYER

None of us would be here if it weren't for Benny Siegel.

LUCKY

I know that, Meyer, you know that... but the truth is... the truth is Benny Siegel is what he is, he don't care if the times change or men change, he's always gonna what he always was. He's got a murderous rage in him, Meyer, it's what made him what he is, what we are. It makes him whole. But he'll never let it go. He can't, it's all he's got.

MEYER

Listen, Lucky, I know you stood up for Benny with the commission, and I appreciate the...

LUCKY

I'd die with that boy, Meyer; but I won't die for him. And neither will you. We both know that.

MEYER

Yeah... *

LUCKY

You and me, Meyer, the tide comes in and we ride it out. Benny, he grabs it by the neck and puts a bullet between its eyes. But the tide, Meyer, if you don't ride with it, eventually it takes you.

MEYER

I know.

LUCKY

Keep an eye on him. I'll do what I can.

MEYER

A good life, Salvatore.

LUCKY

Salut, paisan.

He turns and walks up the gangplank. MEYER stands alone, his head bowed, in the darkness and the approaching fog.

FADE TO

EXT. AIRPORT - DAY

It is a blazing hot day in LA, the sun is beating relentlessly as BUGSY's plane touches down.

CUT TO

EXT. TERMINAL - DAY

BUGSY exits the terminal, dressed to the nines and carrying a single suitcase. A black Cadillac is waiting for him, on which is leaning a short, wiry man with a lined, tough face. His name is MICKEY COHEN. He sees BUGSY and walks up to him.

MICKEY
        Benny Siegel?

BUGSY
        That's me.

MICKEY
        I'm Mickey Cohen, I'm Meyer's man in LA.

BUGSY
        Well, I'm Benny Siegel, now I'm Meyer's man in LA. How you doin'?

They shake hands, MICKEY gestures towards the car.

MICKEY
        I got you booked into the Metropolitan, best hotel in town.

BUGSY
        Exile in style, that's what I like.

MICKEY
        We gotta meeting with Farina at five. You like champagne?

BUGSY
        I like anything.

They get in the car and drive away.

                                                    FADE TO

INT. HOTEL -DAY

BUGSY and MICKEY are walking down the hallway of a fashionable hotel. BUGSY is awkwardly straightening his tie.

MICKEY
        Farina runs the wire out to Kansas City, some of the whorehouses and most of the drug traffic. Everyone thinks that's the coming thing, all the movie stars are snowbirds...

BUGSY
        And the gambling?

MICKEY
        Aint much of it. Most of it's out in Nevada, middle of the desert. They legalized in '33, so the wire services are out there also, connected up to the main lines in town.

BUGSY

Ok.

MICKEY

You got plans for later on?

BUGSY

I'm meeting a friend in a half hour.

MICKEY

A half hour?

BUGSY

Don't worry, this won't take long.

They come to a pair of double doors, MICKEY opens them and WE FOLLOW THEM INTO...

INT. CONFERENCE ROOM - DAY

Four men are seated at the far side of the room, they are TONY FARINA and his lieutenants. BUGSY sits down opposite from them and straightens his tie, MICKEY remains standing behind him.

BUGSY

Salut, Tony.

FARINA

Salut, Benjamin. Your reputation precedes you.

BUGSY

Don't believe everything you hear.

FARINA

If I believed half of what I hear about you, Benny...

BUGSY

I'm here to talk business.

FARINA

So, let's talk business.

BUGSY

The business is this. As of right now, everything you own belongs to us, the whores and the wire and the gambling and the Hollywood snow trade. Every dime and every dollar you make goes through us first.

There is dead silence in the room.

BUGSY

I'm not here to negotiate, gentlemen.

FARINA

What are you here to do?

BUGSY

To give you the gold watch. You're out, all of you. If you play nice, you'll get a piece of the pie, probably bigger than you ever seen in your life, but New York runs things from now on. Which means I run things from now on.

FARINA

And if we don't play nice?

BUGSY smiles, then gets up and loosens his tie again.

BUGSY

It was nice talkin' to you boys.

He gets up and leaves the room. MICKEY stares after him, shocked.

CUT TO

INT. HOTEL LOBBY - DAY

BUGSY walks out and sees a tall, thin man with broad shoulders standing at the doors of the hotel, signing autographs for a pair of excited teenagers. He is GEORGE RAFT, the movie star. BUGSY walks up behind him.

BUGSY

Stick 'em up.

RAFT

Benny, you never change.

He turns and they embrace.

RAFT

How are you, you crazy Jew bastard?

BUGSY

Gettin' better, Georgele. How's the movie business?

RAFT

Ah, Bogart's killin' me. Aint like the old days. Ever since the Code came in they aint makin' gangster pictures no more.

BUGSY

Hey, tell me the truth, I know "Scarface" was about Capone, but he was really playin' me, right?

RAFT

You just keep on thinkin' that, Benny.

They laugh.

RAFT

C'mon, I got a party lined up, you'll love it.

BUGSY

Dames?

RAFT

>Far as the eye can see.

BUGSY

>That's how I like it.

They walk out through the glass doors.

>>SLOW FADE TO

INT. BALLROOM - NIGHT

It is a wild party in a fashionable Hollywood mansion. A band is playing hot jazz and the room is filled with hundreds of people in the best finery the movie business can buy. RAFT is guiding BUGSY through the crowd, pointing out important people. We see them one by one as they pass by.

RAFT

>That's Louis Mayer, he runs MGM. Made a fuckin' fortune on "Gone With the Wind."

BUGSY

>How much?

RAFT

>Word on the street: fifty million dollars.

BUGSY

>I'm in the wrong business.

RAFT

>You said it, Benny. This is the real money. Dreams and plastic, that's all it is, and the people just throw their last nickel and dime at it.

BUGSY

>Better than craps flingin'.

RAFT laughs.

RAFT

>Aint too far away. That's Clark Gable, he's on contract to Mayer. Old bastard's got him by the balls. That's Tom Schillman, he runs most of the subsidiary unions, lighting, cameramen, extras, all that.

There is a spark of interest in BUGSY's eye.

BUGSY

>Oh yeah?

RAFT

>That's Louella Parsons, she writes the gossip column for Hearst. You don't wanna get on her bad side.

BUGSY

>Too late, I'm on everybody's bad side.

RAFT

That's Irving Thalberg, he's head of production for Mayer.

BUGSY

I feel like I'm back in the neighborhood. There's a Jew on every corner.

RAFT

Yeah, we got this place wrapped up pretty tight, even though they're all scared to death someone'll figure out they aint Episcopalians.

BUGSY laughs.

BUGSY

Wait'll they get a load of me.

A PHOTOGRAPHER jumps out of the crowd and points his camera at BUGSY.

PHOTOGRAPHER

Hey, Bugsy!

In a lightening quick move, BUGSY grabs the camera and smashes it to the floor. He grabs the PHOTOGRAPHER by the scruff of the neck. BUGSY's face is contorted with explosive rage.

BUGSY

What did you call me?

PHOTOGRAPHER

Jesus!

BUGSY

Do you know what a bug is? A bug is an insect! Do I look like a fuckin' insect to you!?

PHOTOGRAPHER

I'm sorry! Jesus, I'm sorry!

RAFT

(Under his breath) Benny, it's ok, it's ok. Let him go. This aint the place.

BUGSY releases the trembling PHOTOGRAPHER. He hands him a hundred dollar bill for the camera.

BUGSY

I got my eye on you.

The man slinks away.

RAFT

Jesus, Benny. You gotta watch yourself out here. You sneeze and the next day it's in the papers.

BUGSY straightens his suit.

BUGSY

I'm alright. He just riled me is all.

RAFT looks at him worriedly.

RAFT
>Alright, calm down. Wait here, get yourself a drink. I got someone who wants to meet you.

He disappears into the crowd. BUGSY straightens his tie and takes a glass of champagne from a passing waiter. He downs it in a single gulp and wipes the sweat off his face with his sleeve.

RAFT emerges from the crowd with a stunning, platinum blonde bombshell on his arm. It is JEAN HARLOW, the movie star. She smiles as she sees BUGSY. BUGSY's eyes widen as he sees, as we do, that beneath the dyed hair and the plastic surgery she is DEBORAH from Judy's whorehouse.

RAFT
>Benny, I'm sure you know Miss Jean Harlow, star of "Hell's Angels"?

JEAN holds out her hand.

JEAN
>Mr. Siegel.

BUGSY
>Miss Harlow.

He kisses her hand.

JEAN
>George, would you be a darling and let Mr. Siegel and me take a little stroll on the balcony?

RAFT smiles.

RAFT
>Sure.

She holds out her arm for BUGSY.

JEAN
>Mr. Siegel?

BUGSY takes her arm and they walk out of the crowd on to the balcony.

FADE TO

EXT. BALCONY -NIGHT

JEAN HARLOW and BUGSY walk along the stone balcony of the mansion. Below them, the lights of LA are shining in the night like a galaxy of distant stars.

JEAN
>You've come up in the world, Benny.

BUGSY

So have you, "Jean." I remember you when you were just Debbie Lefkowitz from Mott Street. Best whore in the whole Lower East side. You made somethin' of yourself since you popped the little man's cherry.

JEAN

Don't be disgusting, Benjamin. I left Debbie Lefkowitz back in New York a long time ago.

BUGSY

Don't worry, Debeleh, I won't snitch.

JEAN

I'm sure you won't. You were always the most honest punk I ever knew. You've acquired quite a reputation, you know. I don't think there's a single crime reporter in Hollywood who doesn't know Benny Siegel's in town.

BUGSY

Yeah, well, don't believe everything you hear.

She smiles up at him.

JEAN

With you, Benny, I believe everything I hear.

He laughs.

JEAN

It was sad about Dutch... and Lepkele.

BUGSY

Yeah. Well, that's the game we play. Nobody forced 'em to roll the dice.

JEAN

I think about them, sometimes. (Pause.) Sometimes, it feels like they were just characters out of a storybook.

BUGSY

Like one of your movies.

JEAN

When you look out at these lights, you can believe it.

She stops and looks down at the lights of LA. Then she looks up at the night sky.

JEAN

My God, it's been so long since I've looked at the stars.

Pause.

JEAN

I'm glad you came, Benny.

BUGSY smiles.

BUGSY

Hey, Debeleh, how about we take a little stroll upstairs, for old times' sake?

She laughs.

JEAN

    For me, Benny, there are no old times.

They smile at each other.

                    CUT TO

INT. UPSTAIRS BEDROOM -NIGHT

JEAN and BUGSY are violently making love on a large canopy bed.

JEAN

    Jesus, Benny, you learned a few things since I knew you!

BUGSY

    You taught me everything I know, Debele...

JEAN

    Oh shit, Benny, shut the fuck up!

She shrieks as she comes. He finishes a moment later and rolls off of her. JEAN wipes the sweat off her face.

JEAN

    Welcome to LA, Benjamin.

BUGSY

    It's a hell of a town.

JEAN smiles. She caresses his chin.

JEAN

    And you're gonna paint it red, aint you? Bleed it dry?

BUGSY

    (Smirking) Somethin' like that.

JEAN

    Oh, Benny. You never change.

BUGSY

    Best thing about me.

She smiles again and rolls on to her side next to him.

JEAN

    You're an honest thief, Benny. I always liked that about you.

BUGSY

    I aint no thief, honey, I'm a businessman.

They both laugh.

BUGSY
> Hey, how'd you get into this business anyways?

JEAN
> Oh, I came out here looking for work as an extra. You know, backup dancer, a face in the crowd in the big scenes. But I couldn't get a union card. So... I decided to become a movie star.

She smiles again. Her radiant, bombshell smile.

BUGSY
> (Smiling) Just like that, huh?

JEAN
> Yeah. Well, you can't do shit in this business without a union card. 'Less you wanna be a star.

BUGSY
> You don't say...

CUT TO

INT. DARK ROOM - NIGHT

A fist lands on the jaw of SCHILLMAN, the union delegate. Blood spurts from his mouth. We PULL BACK and see that he is tied to a chair. MICKEY COHEN is working him over. BUGSY is seated on a stool in the corner.

BUGSY
> Alright Mickey, that's enough.

SCHILLMAN spits up blood and coughs.

SCHILLMAN
> Jesus Christ! Who the fuck are you people?!

BUGSY
> I'm New York, you stupid cunt.

He leans forward.

BUGSY
> Here's the deal, my friend. From now on fifty cents on every dollar you get on extras comes to me. Nobody works in the dream factory till I get paid, understand?

SCHILLMAN
> Fuck you, I paid off Farina last month!

BUGSY nods to MICKEY, who punches SCHILLMAN again.

BUGSY
> Alright, that's enough.

He gets up and walks over to SCHILLMAN.

BUGSY
    Farina aint king around here no more. I am.

SCHILLMAN
    We'll see what he says about that.

BUGSY just smiles and pats him on the cheek.

BUGSY
    Clean him up and send him home boys. He's got a lot to think about.

He walks out the door.

                                        CUT TO

EXT. ITALIAN RESTAURANT - NIGHT

FARINA and his boys are walking out towards a waiting taxi. SCHILLMAN is with them. His face is bruised and bandaged.

FARINA
    What do I pay you for, Schillman? You can't even handle your own fucking people!

SCHILLMAN
    This is New York muscle, Farina! What am I supposed to do?

FARINA
    To do? We had a deal. I keep New York off your back, you keep the sheenies off mine! What happened to integrity in business? Whole damn country's going to hell!

SCHILLMAN
    I...

FARINA
    Fuck it. I gotta meeting in New York next week. After that, that Jew bastard aint gonna be nothin' to worry about. No offense.

The taxi door opens and as FARINA turns to get in, we see BUGSY and MICKEY COHEN in the back seat.

They level their tommy-guns and OPEN FIRE, mowing down FARINA and his boys. Only SHILLMAN is left standing.

As SCHILLMAN stands there, frozen with shock, BUGSY gives him a half smile and closes the taxi door. The taxi drives away, leaving SCHILLMAN alone with the carnage.

                                        CUT TO

MONTAGE - BUGSY TAKES OVER LA.

- A movie set, a musical with a large crowd and a chorus of dancers. We travel past the assembled crowd to the side of the soundstage, where a still bandaged SCHILLMAN hands MICKEY COHEN a suitcase.

- A wire service backroom being smashed to pieces by BUGSY's boys. We travel to the side and see an accountant, with MICKEY COHEN's knife to his throat, handing MICKEY a large wad of bills.

- A massive Hollywood party, JEAN HARLOW and BUGSY are dancing to hot jazz.

- A drug dealer's pad. BUGSY is holding a gun to the dealer's head as his boys rip open packets of cocaine and spill them out on to the floor.

- Cops taking pictures of a crime scene, five dead gangsters are laid out in a line in a fashionable nightclub.

- MICKEY COHEN stowing cash underneath his mattress.

- BUGSY and JEAN HARLOW dancing, she is smiling her bombshell smile.

- BUGSY shaking hands with LOUIS MAYER as the cameras flash.

- BUGSY and GEORGE RAFT drinking in a fashionable whorehouse, girls on their laps.

- MICKEY COHEN cleaning his gun.

- BUGSY and JEAN dancing. The band finishes their song on a single, warbling not, and the lights fade down to BLACK as if on a soundstage.

FADE IN

INT. HOTEL LOBBY -NIGHT

MEYER is talking on the phone in a dimly lit hotel. A sign behind him reads "WELCOME TO HAVANA" in Spanish and English.

MEYER
> Benny, you killed a made guy! He had a meeting in New York set for last Tuesday! The wops are bleeding from the fuckin' eyes on this one!

BUGSY
> You can handle 'em, Meyer. You always have.

MEYER
> Benny, I sent you out there to make money, not to overturn the fuckin' world.

BUGSY
> You don't send me no place, little man! I came out here to build the new world, and that's what I'm doing. Farina was an obstacle, sooner or later we woulda had to remove it. I just did it sooner not later.

MEYER
> Benny, it was a decision we all should have made.

BUGSY
> Meyer, am I boss out here or not?

MEYER

Benny, you are part of an organization.

BUGSY

That organization is in New York and Havana. I'm here. Me.

MEYER

Benny...

BUGSY

Come on, Meyer, the money's flowing like water over here.

MEYER

Yeah, and that's the only thing that...

BUGSY

The only thing that what?

MEYER

You better keep the money flowing, Benny. That's all.

BUGSY

Little man, you worry too much.

MEYER hangs up slowly and turns to the side. LUCKY is sitting next to him, smoking a cigarette. MEYER shrugs his shoulders. LUCKY says nothing. He taps his cigarette into the ivory ashtray in front of him.

                                                              CUT TO

INT. BUGSY'S HOTEL SUITE - NIGHT

BUGSY has just hung up the phone. He straightens his tie and puts on his jacket. GEORGE RAFT comes out of the other room.

RAFT

C'mon Benny, you're holding up the works.

BUGSY

Business, Georgele.

RAFT

Yeah, you're all business. C'mon, you look like a movie star. Let's go.

They walk out of the suite.

                                                              CUT TO

INT. BALLROOM - NIGHT

Another huge Hollywood blowout. Stars, reporters, and party-goers dance and mingle around the huge ballroom. RAFT, BUGSY, and JEAN HARLOW are standing to the side, drinking champagne.

JEAN

I hear you're making quite a name for yourself around town, Benny.

BUGSY
    Yeah, well...

JEAN
    Don't believe everything I hear?

BUGSY
    Maybe half of it.

She laughs.

JEAN
    I'm in the wrong business, aint I, Benny?

BUGSY
    You got that right.

A PHOTOGRAPHER pops out of the crowd.

PHOTOGRAPHER
    Miss Harlow!

They turn, and the PHOTOGRAPHER stops dead, it is the same man BUGSY assaulted.

PHOTOGRAPHER
    Mr. Siegel, I'm sorry...

BUGSY
    It's alright, go ahead.

The PHOTOGRAPHER doesn't move a muscle.

BUGSY
    Don't worry, I aint gonna kill you. We only kill each other.

He smiles. The PHOTOGRAPHER takes his picture and slinks away.

JEAN
    Fucking vultures.

RAFT
    They're just trying to make a buck, Jeannie, like the rest of us.

BUGSY
    I know he's in the wrong business. I wouldn't wanna antagonize a guy like me.

They laugh. Suddenly, they hear yelling from the other side of the room. They turn to look and see:

A man and a woman arguing. The woman is ravishingly beautiful, but with something cheap, even wanton, about her. She throws a glass of champagne in the man's face and slaps him. He stalks away.

BUGSY looks at her, mesmerized.

RAFT
You alright, Benny?

BUGSY
Who is that?

JEAN
You're still a greenhorn, Benny. That is Miss Virginia Hill.

BUGSY
Who is she? What does she do?

JEAN

Nothing. She *is*. You should go talk to her, Benny. I think she's the only one in this room with a rep worse than yours.

BUGSY puts down his glass and we PULL BACK as he pushes his way through the crowd, until he finds himself next to VIRGINIA at the drinks table. She is lighting a cigarette. She looks at him absentmindedly, and then turns away.

BUGSY
Can I buy you a drink?

VIRGINIA
No.

BUGSY
Why not?

VIRGINIA
Here the drinks are free.

She takes a glass of champagne off the table and downs it.

BUGSY
I'm Benny Siegel.

VIRGINIA
I know. They call you "Bugsy."

BUGSY
Nobody calls me that.

VIRGINIA
Maybe I do.

BUGSY just stares at her, dumbfounded.

VIRGINIA
So what do you want, Mr. Siegel? Dance, conversation, pussy?

He cannot answer for a long moment.

BUGSY
How about a dance?

VIRGINIA
    I hate dancing.

BUGSY
    So do I.

VIRGINIA smiles for the first time.

VIRGINIA
    Good.

                                     CUT TO

INT. BUGSY'S SUITE -NIGHT

VIRGINIA enters the room, a cigarette still burning down in her hand. BUGSY follows her at a slight distance, fascinated, eyeing her like a panther. She turns to him and looks at him suspiciously for a long moment, leaning on the writing desk.

VIRGINIA
    You got an ashtray?

He takes one from the bedside table and puts in on the desk behind her, brushing her arm as he does so. He does not move back, but stands inches away from her, looking down into her eyes. She stubs out the cigarette.

VIRGINIA
    Nice place.

BUGSY
    Best that money can buy.

She smiles.

VIRGINIA
    Lot of money in your line of work, isn't there?

BUGSY advances on her, backing her up towards a small night table in the corner.

BUGSY
    There's some.

VIRGINIA
    That's not what I hear.

BUGSY
    Don't believe everything you hear.

VIRGINIA
    Whyever not?

BUGSY
    It might not be true.

VIRGINIA
     In my experience it usually is.

She bumps up against the night table and stops.

VIRGINIA
     So, is it true what they say about Jew girls?

BUGSY
     What's that?

VIRGINIA
     You know. That they teach their boys to do it the right way.

BUGSY
     (Smiling) Don't believe everything you hear.

VIRGINIA
     Don't worry. I always try to find out for myself.

They stare at each other for a long moment.

VIRGINIA
     Well? What are you waiting for, a written invitation?

BUGSY grabs her by the shoulders and pushes her down on the night table. He pins her wrists above her head with one hand and rips her panties off with the other. He hitches her dress up and starts ferociously fucking her.

VIRGINIA
     C'mon, is that the best you can do?!

He lets out an animal grunt and pulls her head back by the hair. VIRGINIA shrieks with approval, wrapping her legs around him. BUGSY's knuckles are white against her wrists. She bites her lip and pushes her hips up against him as he pounds at her. Suddenly, BUGSY covers her face with his hand and exhales loudly as he finishes. Breathing hard, he straightens up and rearranges himself.

VIRGINIA gets up slowly from the table, runs her hand through her hair and smoothes out her wrinkled dress.

VIRGINIA
     Well, you got potential. I'll give you that.

She walks to the door. As she leaves, she turns back and looks at BUGSY.

VIRGINIA
     Don't be a stranger.

She leaves, closing the door behind her. BUGSY stands alone in the middle of the room, open-mouthed with amazement.

                                                            CUT TO

INT. HOTEL LOBBY -NIGHT

BUGSY and MICKEY are coming in the glass doors, MICKEY is talking excitedly.

MICKEY

C'mon Benny, this is ridiculous, I'm getting calls three times a day from New York. You gotta tell 'em somethin'.

BUGSY

I'll get back to 'em when I'm good and ready.

MICKEY

Benny, this aint smart.

BUGSY

What are they gonna do, Mickey? They're out there, I'm out here, what the fuck are they gonna do?

MICKEY looks uncomfortable.

MICKEY

This aint smart, Benny.

BUGSY

Mickey, go home. Stop worrying, you're gonna give yourself a heart attack.

MICKEY

Aint me I'm worried about, Benny.

BUGSY

Go home, Mickey.

MICKEY exhales in a frustrated tone and turns away. BUGSY walks to the front desk.

BUGSY

My key, please.

CLERK

Of course, Mr. Siegel. (He hands BUGSY the key.) Your friend is waiting for you.

BUGSY

My friend?

CLERK

Yes, sir. He arrived an hour ago. He said you were expecting him.

BUGSY

Oh, yeah...of course.

BUGSY walks purposefully towards the elevators.

CUT TO

EXT. HALLWAY - NIGHT

BUGSY is standing in front of his door. He takes his pistol out of his waistband. Holding it along his leg, he unlocks the door and goes in.

CUT TO

INT. BUGSY'S SUITE - NIGHT

A figure is seated in an easy chair with his back to the door, smoking a cigarette.

VOICE
      Is that you Benny?

BUGSY advances slowly into the room. We REVERSE ANGLE and see that the figure seated in the chair is none other than MOESY SEDWAY, looking haggard and worn. He seems to be on the verge of tears.

BUGSY
      Yeah, it's me.

MOESY
      How are you, Benny?

BUGSY rounds the chair, and his eyes open wide as he sees MOESY.

BUGSY
      Jesus, Moe.

MOESY
      Yeah, it's me.

BUGSY puts his gun away and sits across from MOESY.

BUGSY
      Moe... holy shit... where you been?

MOESY
      Around. Middle of the country, mostly. Tryin' to stay outta sight.

BUGSY
      Jesus, Moe, you look like hell.

MOESY
      Thanks.

He laughs, but it comes out like a sob.

BUGSY
      What are you doin' here, Moesy?

MOESY
      I couldn't hack it no more out there, Benny. No friends. My wife... I just... just couldn't hack it no more. I just got tired, Benny, I got so tired. You understand?

BUGSY

    Yeah. Yeah, I understand.

MOESY wipes his eyes with his sleeves.

BUGSY

    Listen, Moesy, I gotta make a call. Business, you know? Don't go no place, ok?

MOESY nods. BUGSY gets up and goes into the next room. We HOLD for a moment on MOESY's face, crumpled with years of loneliness and grief.

                                              CUT TO

INT. BUGSY'S KITCHEN

BUGSY is talking on the phone. MEYER is on the other end of the line.

MEYER

    Jesus Christ, where the fuck has he been?

BUGSY

    The Midwest somewhere, I think. Sounds like he's been driftin' all over the place. Tryin' to stay out of sight.

MEYER

    My God. Ten years in the Midwest'd drive anybody crazy.

BUGSY

    What do you wanna do with this, Meyer?

Pause.

MEYER

    Benny, you know the score here.

BUGSY

    He aint the same man, Meyer. You should see him. He's like a little kid. He just sits there bawlin' his eyes out.

MEYER

    Benny, I can't...

BUGSY

    Meyer, this aint no two-bit stoolie. This is...

MEYER

    Benny, I feel the same way, but...this is the game. He knew the rules.

BUGSY

    Meyer...

MEYER

    Benny, you take care of this and... it'll solve a lot of your problems with New York. That's all I'm saying.

CUT TO

INT. LIVING ROOM

MOESY is still sitting in his chair. He wipes his eyes. BUGSY comes back into the room.

BUGSY
> Hey, Moe, let's get out of here, alright? Some place we can talk private. These walls have ears, know what I mean?

MOESY
> Sure Benny, I'll get my coat.

He gets out of his chair unsteadily and starts putting his coat on. There is a knock at the door.

BUGSY gestures to MOESY to go to the other room, then he opens the door. VIRGINIA is standing in the hall.

VIRGINIA
> Hello, Benjamin.

BUGSY
> Ginny, you should have called first.

VIRGINIA
> What, you don't like surprises?

BUGSY
> I gotta friend here.

VIRGINIA
> Good, you can introduce me. Is she pretty?

She pushes past him into the room. She sees MOESY standing in the shadows.

VIRGINIA
> Hello.

BUGSY
> Virginia Hill, this is Moesy Sedway. He's from the old neighborhood.

VIRGINIA
> It's always a pleasure to meet one of Benjamin's fellow hoodlums.

MOESY looks confused.

BUGSY
> Look, Ginny, me and Moe got business to discuss. We'll be back in an hour or so.

VIRGINIA
> I'm an impatient girl, Benjamin. Don't make me wait too long.

CUT TO

EXT. CLIFFTOP - NIGHT

BUGSY's car pulls to a stop on a promontory overlooking Los Angeles. BUGSY and MOESY clamber out and walk slowly through the tall grass and weeds. Towards the edge of the cliff.

We CRANE UPWARDS TILTING DOWN, revealing below them the glowing expanse of Los Angeles stretching off into the horizon.

MOESY

  My God, Benny. It's beautiful.

BUGSY

  Yeah. Yeah it is, aint it?

BUGSY stands behind MOESY, pulling up his collar against the wind.

BUGSY

  I never did like the cold.

MOESY

  (Chuckling) Yeah. Yeah, I remember. You was always like that. (He suddenly becomes emotional, his voice choked.) We come a long way, aint we, Benny?

BUGSY

  (Almost whispering) Yeah. Yeah, I guess we have.

MOESY

  A long way to go to no place at all. You know what I mean?

BUGSY

  (Tears glisten in his eyes.) Yeah. Yeah I do.

MOESY

  I never meant to do nothin' to hurt you boys. You was always like brothers to me. You know that.

BUGSY

  Yeah. Yeah Moesy, I know.

MOESY

  I just... you know... I didn't have no choice.

BUGSY points his pistol at the back of MOESY's head.

MOESY

  I'm sorry, Benny.

BUGSY

  It's alright, Moesy. Don't worry about it. Don't worry about anything.

BUGSY FIRES into the back of his friend's head. MOESY collapses in a heap at his feet.

LOW ANGLE SHOT in SLOW MOTION of BUGSY as he EMPTIES HIS GUN into MOESY's body, then kicks it unceremoniously over the edge and into the gully.

                    CUT TO

INT. BUGSY'S HOTEL ROOM -NIGHT

BUGSY comes in the door. Virginia is already in sheer lingerie. She looks confused.

VIRGINIA
> Where's your friend?

HE SMACKS HER ACROSS THE FACE with his open hand. She gasps in shock. Her nose gushes blood on to her expensive dress.

BUGSY
> Don't ever fuckin' ask me that again!

BUGSY takes off his coat and unbuttons his vest. He places his gun on the dresser and starts undoing his cufflinks. VIRGINA stands there looking at him, her blood running through her fingers.

She scoops up the lamp from the writing desk and SMASHES BUGSY IN THE BACK OF THE HEAD with it. BUGSY doubles over in pain, holding his head and moaning.

VIRGINIA
> You fucking Jew bastard! Don't ever hit me again!

BUGSY shrieks like an animal and PUNCHES HER IN THE FACE, sending her sprawling across the room. She throws her purse at him as he comes at her and scrambles to her feet. Blood running anew down the front of her face, SHE KICKS HIM SQUARE IN THE CROTCH. He collapses on to the floor and crumples into a fetal position. SHE KICKS HIM IN THE STOMACH.

He grabs her by the ankle and trips her up. Still doubled over, he gets to his feet, takes his gun from the dresser and straddles her, holding the gun in her face.

VIRGINIA
> Go ahead! I aint afraid of you!

She spits in his face. He wipes it away unceremoniously, lowers the gun and gets off of her.

She gets to her feet and then PUNCHES HIM VICIOUSLY IN THE SOLAR PLEXUS. He TACKLES HER and they sprawl across the room, knocking over furniture, smashing the room to pieces. We hear smashing glass and falling objects.

FADE TO

LATER

The two of them are wrapped in each other's arms amidst the remains of the room. They are both bleeding and bruised.

VIRGINIA
> I love you.

BUGSY cradles her head in his arms.

CUT TO

INT. HALLWAY - DAY

MICKEY COHEN is knocking furiously at the door to BUGSY's room. Finally, BUGSY opens it, looking tired and bleary-eyed.

BUGSY
        What is it?

MICKEY looks in at the destroyed room. VIRGINIA is asleep, naked, on the bed.

MICKEY
        Quite a party last night, huh?

BUGSY
        What do you want, Mickey?

MICKEY
        We was supposed to hit the road a half hour ago, check out the Vegas wire.

BUGSY
        Shit, I forgot.

MICKEY
        You forgot?

BUGSY
        Give me a minute, Mickey.

MICKEY
        Benny...

BUGSY
        Give me a minute.

He slams the door shut. MICKEY, almost at the end of his patience, looks at his watch.

                                                        CUT TO

INT. MICKEY'S CAR - DAY

MICKEY and BUGSY are driving through the Nevada desert. BUGSY is slumped in the passenger seat, exhausted, dozing behind his sunglasses.

MICKEY
        Dame wearin' you out?

BUGSY
        None of your business.

MICKEY
        Relax, Benny, just curious is all. She's got herself quite a rep around town.

BUGSY

So do I.

MICKEY

Aint that the truth.

BUGSY

What's that mean?

MICKEY

Nothin', Benny, nothin'. You work it out with New York?

BUGSY

Yeah. I straightened it out.

MICKEY

Good. Those fuckers been ridin' me for weeks.

BUGSY

Aint there nothin' but sand out here?

MICKEY laughs.

MICKEY

Not till Utah.

BUGSY

Jesus...

MICKEY

Hell of a place. Man could die out here and once the buzzards and the coyotes are done with him, he'd be nothin' but white bones in the desert.

CUT TO

INT. VEGAS SALOON - DAY

It is almost noon. The sun is blazing. The heat is palpable. It rises in waves off the asphalt highway. MICKEY and BUGSY enter the small highway saloon. There is nothing inside but the bar and a few slot machines. In their finely tailored suits, they look completely out of place. A sign on the wall reads "BLUE FLAMINGO SALOON - BEER AND WINE ONLY". A few natives are dozing by the bar. A pair of old men in cowboy hats are playing cards near the window.

BUGSY

Jesus. Deadest slot joint I ever saw.

MICKEY

Yeah, nobody wants to come out to the middle of the desert. Some of the whorehouses in Reno do alright, but the wire's the only thing here makes any money. Let's talk to Fred.

BUGSY

You talk to him. I'm gonna take a walk.

MICKEY

You're gonna what?

BUGSY

A walk, Mickey. I'm gonna take a walk. Go talk to him.

MICKEY, totally exasperated, says nothing. He disappears into the back room. BUGSY walks out on to the sun-drenched highway.

CUT TO

EXT. DESERT - DAY

BUGSY walks slowly across the highway, squinting behind his sunglasses. At the other side, there is nothing but a broad expanse of rocky desert stretching out to the horizon. The wind whispers in the background.

LOW ANGLE of BUGSY as he looks around. He kicks lightly at the rocky sand beneath his feet. Slowly, we CLOSE IN on him, until we see nothing but an EXTREME CLOSEUP of his face framed against the primordial landscape.

CUT TO

INT. CAR - DAY

It is late afternoon. BUGSY and MICKEY are driving back, the desert disappearing behind them.

BUGSY

Mickey, when we get back I want you to call the little man. Tell him to fly out here tomorrow night.

MICKEY

What's up, boss?

BUGSY

I think I just had a vision.

MICKEY looks at him sideways. Then he chuckles.

MICKEY

Jesus. Two hours in the desert and he thinks he's Moses.

BUGSY doesn't respond. He stares out the window at the never ending sand.

CUT TO

EXT. AIRPORT TERMINAL - DAY

MEYER is walking out of the terminal, carrying his suitcases. BUGSY is waiting by his car, MICKEY COHEN at the wheel. He walks up to MEYER and embraces him.

BUGSY

Good to see you, little man. How are you?

MEYER

Tired.

BUGSY

You can sleep in the car.

MEYER

The what?

BUGSY takes his suitcases and throws them in the trunk.

BUGSY

C'mon, we're goin' for a ride.

MEYER looks puzzled. But he gets in and they drive away.

FADE TO

EXT. VEGAS HIGHWAY - DAY

BUGSY's car pulls to a stop across from the Blue Flamingo Saloon. He and MEYER get out and BUGSY leads him into the desert.

MEYER

Alright, Benny, you stumped me. What am I lookin' at?

BUGSY

Meyer, you are looking at the future site of the biggest hotel and casino in the country.

MEYER

Benny, we're in the middle of the fuckin' desert.

BUGSY

Look around you, Meyer, what do you see?

MEYER

Sand.

BUGSY

Let me tell you what I see. I see a four lane highway running from LA to Salt Lake City, straight through, no tolls. I see a place with cheap land, and a lot of it. I see a place with casinos and whorehouses that don't never get raided by the feds. And over that hill... (He points into the distance.) I see LA, and behind it, California. Twenty million people with more money than France and England put together and nothin' to spend it on.

MEYER

It's finally happened, Benny. You've gone nuts.

BUGSY

C'mon little man. You was always the one with the brains. Think! This is what we've been lookin' for! A license to do what we do. With the DA and the governor and the goddam president in our corner. Everyone plays, everyone pays, and everything innocent and legal. Jesus, Meyer, we'll be bigger than General Motors.

MEYER

Benny, we're already bigger than General Motors.

BUGSY

Meyer, I'm talking about a place that's mine, outright. A place they can look at and say: Benny Siegel was here. He took a pile of dirt in the middle of nowhere and built something! A place that'll say: he was real! He was here! He wasn't no punk Jew boy! Look at what he made! For himself!

MEYER

For us, Benny?

BUGSY

You know what I'm talkin' about Meyer. A place that's ours, our own! Without the middlemen and the payoffs and the parasites and the Italians with their hands in everyone's pocket, gettin' fat off the money we made 'em!

MEYER

Benny...

BUGSY

This is what I'm offering you, Meyer: No cops, no wops, no Deweys, no Roosevelts, no Kefauvers, no fucking Moustache Petes. Just us. Our own.

MEYER

Benny, the decision's been made. We already started moving everything to Havana...

BUGSY

Havana! Havana's the other side of the world! They don't even speak English! You think folks are gonna fly across the ocean just to hit some slots?

MEYER

I told you, Benny, the high rollers go where the game is.

BUGSY

Yeah, well I'm not talkin' about the high rollers. The war's over Meyer! People got money to burn! People are gonna be buying cars and houses and stores! They're not gonna pack up to some Spanish shithole for a month just to throw down on the house! I'm talking about the shop owners with the week's earnings. The lawyers and dentists and doctors lookin' to spend away the good life. The gas station attendant who's gonna blow the week's paycheck and his wife's grocery money. Meyer, who needs the high rollers? Every sucker in the country, every sucker in the world, is gonna be lining up to throw money in our pockets. And they'll drive an hour through the desert to do it. I know it and you know it.

MEYER looks at the wasteland around him, squinting in the blinding sun. Finally he looks back up at BUGSY.

MEYER

What are you gonna call it?

BUGSY smiles his big, toothy punk's smile.

BUGSY

The Flamingo.

CUT TO

MONTAGE - BUILDING THE FLAMINGO

- BUGSY supervising the trucks and backhoes as they clear the desert away.

- Customers at the Blue Flamingo Saloon looking out at the scene, utterly dumbfounded.

- Contractors showing BUGSY samples for the casino walls. BUGSY looks over at VIRGINIA, she points to one and smiles. He smiles back and kisses her on the cheek.

- BUGSY celebrating with GEORGE RAFT and JEAN HARLOW.

BUGSY
        Hey Jean, you know Judy Garland? Does she still do shows?

JEAN
        For you, Benny, I'm sure.

- Lights being placed in front of the newly built facade of the hotel. A giant sign is being raised into place, it reads: "FLAMINGO HOTEL AND CASINO - GRAND OPENING IN TWO MONTHS."

-VIRGINIA and BUGSY watching women model possible uniforms for the hat check girls. VIRGINIA turns to BUGSY and smiles salaciously.

-VIRGINIA on top of BUGSY, furiously fucking him. BUGSY is holding his pistol against her chin.

VIRGINIA
        You want to kill me, don't you, tough guy?

He clicks back the hammer and she shrieks with pleasure.

- BUGSY showing the GOVERNOR OF NEVADA around the site. The GOVERNOR smiles and shakes BUGSY's hand. Flashbulbs pop.

- The Flamingo's sign being fixed into place. It now reads "GRAND OPENING IN FOUR MONTHS."

- BUGSY talking with two nightclub singers. He hands them two contracts. They look at MICKEY COHEN, who is glowering at them over BUGSY's shoulder and sign.

- BUGSY inspecting the interior of the casino. The laborers are hard at work.

- A series of images of money and suitcases full of money changing hands.

- The sign on the facade now reads "GRAND OPENING IN SIX MONTHS."

- The lights of the Flamingo turned on full blast in the desert night.

- CLOSE UP of BUGSY'S FACE. The red Flamingo sign lights up his face, then fades away to BLACK.

FADE IN

INT. HAVANA HOTEL ROOM - DAY

A gathering of bosses. They are seated around a conference table. We hear Cuban music from outside the windows where the sun is shining through palm trees, making the room appear even darker than it is. MEYER, LUCKY, and LUCKY's lieutenant, FRANK COSTELLO, are seated around the head of the table. One of the BOSSES is examining a piece of paper. He throws it on the table.

BOSS #1

He's completely out of his goddam mind.

LUCKY

Antonio, this is business. There's no need for that kind of language.

BOSS #1

He's spent three million already! And still no opening date! Always another month, another two months, another six months! We're pouring money down a hole in the fucking desert!

BOSS #2

And my boys in LA tell me he's gettin' robbed blind on the costs. Kickbacks, payoffs, poor materials, poor workmanship... The union's settling its debts on our backs! And the politicians! The governor's gonna buy himself a new mansion on our dime!

LUCKY

That's right, our dime. All of us. And the last time I checked me and the little man was still running this syndicate.

BOSS #1

All respect, Lucky, but somethin's gotta be done.

BOSS #3

It gets worse. I hear that girlfriend he's got gets on a plane to Switzerland every two weeks, with three suitcases full of money.

There is a murmur around the table.

MEYER

Where did you hear that?

BOSS #3

I got my sources.

MEYER

That's a lie. I know Benny. He's as straight as they come in our business.

BOSS #1

That kid's got a screw loose, Meyer. He always has! Now you're lettin' that crazy Jew bastard run around like a drunk on payday! With our money!

MEYER stands up, for the first time we see him truly enraged.

MEYER

You listen to me you prick! You wouldn't be nothin' if it weren't for Benny Siegel! None of us would! You'd still be on Mott Street pickin' the meatballs out of your ass! That crazy Jew bastard made you all rich! He gave you everything you have! And for that I have to listen to you call him a thief behind his back! Everything you have, everything I have..!

LUCKY puts his hand on MEYER's arm.

LUCKY

Meyer, calm down. No one is accusing Benny of anything. I love him like a brother, you know that. But you gotta admit, we gotta problem here.

BOSS #1

Yeah, a problem you signed off on.

BOSS #2

Without consulting us.

LUCKY

We all signed off on it! And I got faith in this investment. 'Cos Meyer's right. Benny Siegel aint never steered me wrong yet. And I owe him a few. We all do. However, I'm sure even Meyer will agree that some of your concerns are... legitimate. So I propose that we send Meyer to LA to assess the situation.

BOSS 1

Yeah, send a Jew to police a Jew...

LUCKY

That's enough! I'm sure we all have confidence in Meyer's opinion. I'd take it over any one of yours.

There is silence in the room.

LUCKY

If there are no objections, this meeting is over.

The BOSSES file out of the room.

LUCKY

Frankie, go have a smoke.

FRANK COSTELLO nods and goes out, shutting the door behind him.

LUCKY

Meyer, you gotta give me something here. I'm doing everything I can but... the sharks are circling.

MEYER

You know Benny...

LUCKY

Yeah, I know Benny. And so do you.

MEYER

You think he's a thief, Charlie?

LUCKY

> No. I think he runs on his gut and not on his head. And that can get anybody in trouble. 'Specially when...women are involved. Women like Virginia Hill. You gotta talk to him Meyer. Make him see what's goin' on. He's been skating on thin ice for years, but this...

MEYER looks at LUCKY with a hard, cold look. Then he relents and nods.

LUCKY

> Good. Salut, paisan.

LUCKY gets up and walks out. MEYER exhales and slumps in his chair.

> FADE TO

EXT. FLAMINGO CONSTRUCTION SITE - DAY

MEYER gets out of his car, sweating bullets in the desert heat. He trudges through the chaos of the construction site until he finds BUGSY looking at samples of statues.

BUGSY

> Yeah, that one for the foyer, and the other one for the blackjack floor. Get rid of the other ones.

The men carry them away.

MEYER

> Benny, we got to talk.

BUGSY

> I'm busy, Meyer.

MEYER

> No you're not.

BUGSY looks at him for the first time, his eyes cold and narrow.

BUGSY

> Alright, I'm not.

> FADE TO

A MOMENT LATER

They are standing a ways off from the site, framed by the enormous landscape of the unspoiled desert.

MEYER

> What the fuck are you doing here, Benny?

BUGSY

> I'm building a hotel, Meyer. What's it look like?

MEYER

> You're five million in the hole already, and you won't even give us an opening date.

BUGSY

I'm clearing ten million a year on white powder alone, and you know it! You owe me this, Meyer!

MEYER

Nobody owes anybody anything, Benny. This is not personal. These are businessmen. I'm a businessman.

BUGSY

No you're not, Meyer. You're a gangster, and so am I. And don't ever forget that.

MEYER

I love you, Benny. That's why I'm gonna tell you this straight. People are watching, and they don't like what they see.

BUGSY

Let 'em talk.

MEYER

It aint just talk this time, Benny.

BUGSY looks MEYER in the eye.

BUGSY

What are you tryin' to tell me, little man?

MEYER

Benny, where does your girlfriend go every two weeks?

BUGSY

What?

MEYER

Every two weeks your girlfriend gets on a plane. Where does she go?

BUGSY

How the hell should I know?

MEYER

You like people to think you're stupid, Benny, but I know different.

BUGSY

You think I'm skimming off the top, little man?

MEYER

I know you're not skimming off the top, but what I know aint important.

BUGSY

You know what we've got here, Meyer! You know what this place could be!

MEYER

Benny, I'm the only thing standing between you and the wrath of God. I've protected you for a long time, because of what I owe you, and because I love you like a brother. Nothing will ever change that. But I'm only human. I can't stand against God forever.

BUGSY says nothing for a long moment, his hands in his pockets.

BUGSY
> Well, do what you gotta do Meyer.

He walks away.

MEYER
> Benny!

But BUGSY has disappeared into the desert.

CUT TO

INT. AIRPORT - NIGHT

MEYER is boarding his plane

CUT TO

INT. CAR - NIGHT

BUGSY is being driven through the dark streets of Los Angeles. There has just been a rainstorm, and the drops on the windows cast shadows like tears on his face.

CUT TO

INT. AIRPLANE - NIGHT

MEYER is writing on some papers, but he can't work. He puts the pen down and sighs.

CUT TO

EXT. STREET - NIGHT

BUGSY pulls up in front of VIRGINIA HILL's house.

CUT TO

INT. AIRPLANE

CLOSE UP of MEYER looking pensively out the window at the lights passing by beneath him.

CUT TO

INT. VIRGINIA'S HOUSE - NIGHT

BUGSY comes in, closing the door softly behind him.

BUGSY
Ginny! You home?

VIRGINIA
I'm in the living room.

BUGSY goes into the living room, where VIRGINIA is steadying a painting on the wall.

VIRGINIA
What do you think?

BUGSY
Yeah, it's nice.

VIRGINIA
You have no eye for art, Benjamin.

BUGSY sits in an easy chair, looking exhausted. VIRGINIA turns to him.

VIRGINIA
Benjamin, you look like shit.

BUGSY
Ginny, where do you go every two weeks?

We CLOSE IN on an EXTREME CLOSE UP of VIRGINIA's face She looks shocked.

CUT TO

INT. MEYER'S APARTMENT - NIGHT

MEYER comes in, putting his coat and briefcase in their usual place.

MEYER
Jenny?

He goes into the kitchen and looks in the refrigerator.

MEYER
Jenny, are the kids asleep?

He goes into the living room. Nobody. The house is dark and empty.

MEYER
Jen?

He goes into the bedroom, looking confused.

JUMP CUT TO

LOW ANGLE SHOT of MEYER opening the closet. He sweeps his clothes aside and sees a line of clothes hangers hanging empty.

He turns and, again from a LOW ANGLE, we see him as he spies an envelope on the dresser. He picks it up. In a woman's hand is written a single word, his own name: MEYER. He looks at it for a moment, turning it over in his hand. Then he rips it in half. On the SOUND, we...

                                                                              CUT TO

INT. VIRGINIA'S HOUSE - NIGHT

CLOSE UP of VIRGINIA. Her eyes are red. She has clearly been crying for a long time.

BUGSY reaches out and puts his hand on her arm.

BUGSY
          It's alright. It's alright. (He sighs.) I'll take care of it.

                                                                              CUT TO

INT. HOTEL SUITE - NIGHT

BUGSY is looking at himself in the mirror. He straightens his tie awkwardly. GEORGE RAFT comes into the frame.

RAFT
          Let me do it, you goddam hoodlum.

He straightens the tie expertly.

RAFT
          You ready?

BUGSY
          Sure.

RAFT
          You nervous?

BUGSY smiles his smile.

BUGSY
          Never.

RAFT
          Let's go.

BUGSY
          You get in touch with Jeannie?

RAFT
          Yeah, she'll meet us there.

BUGSY
          Alright.

He looks at himself in the mirror again; slowly we CLOSE IN on an EXTREME CLOSE UP of his face. For the first time, we see fear in his eyes.

                                                                              FADE TO

INT. FLAMINGO HOTEL - NIGHT

CLOSE UP of BUGSY'S HANDS. He is dealing out cards in a game of solitaire.

WE BEGIN TO PULL BACK and in a SINGLE UNBROKEN SHOT WE CONTINUE BACK through the Flamingo in all its finished, resplendent, gaudy beauty. RAFT and JEAN HARLOW are leaning against the bar, looking pensively at BUGSY. Waiters and slot girls are standing around looking bored. A few well dressed patrons are milling around, doing nothing. Except for them, the place is completely empty.

SLOWLY, we exit the room, and find ourselves outside the hotel, facing the enormous fa.ade we saw under construction. It is drenched by by a blinding desert rainstorm. The sign now reads: "HOTEL FLAMINGO GRAND OPENING!"

                                                                              CUT TO

INT. CONFERENCE ROOM - DAY

It is another gathering of bosses. MEYER and LUCKY are once again at the head of the table, but this time BUGSY is addressing the assembled.

BUGSY
        First, I want to thank you gentlemen for the respect and the support you've given this
        project from the beginning. We've hit a few snags, but I can assure you that, with your
        help, the Flamingo can reopen in ten days. And this time, weather permitting, we can
        start making some serious money. They... uh... they say Hollywood is the dream factory,
        but Las Vegas is no dream, we've made it real. Thank you.

MEYER nods and gestures with his head to the door. BUGSY nods and leaves. There is a long, pregnant pause.

LUCKY
        Can I see a show of hands, gentlemen?

One by one, the BOSSES raise their hands.

LUCKY
        Meyer?

MEYER looks at the table, his head bent.

LUCKY
        Meyer?

MEYER barely raises his head.

MEYER
        There's only one thing to do with a man who steals from his friends.

CUT TO

INT. HALLWAY - DAY

MEYER comes out and sees BUGSY waiting alone in the dark hallway. BUGSY turns to him expectantly as he approaches.

MEYER
>They're gonna give you the money.

BUGSY smiles.

BUGSY
>I knew you could pull it off, little man.

He holds out his hand. MEYER begins to shake it, but then pulls BUGSY to him and embraces him. BUGSY looks embarrassed.

MEYER
>Take care of yourself, Benny.

BUGSY
>I always do, little man.

MEYER
>I know.

BUGSY
>See you in two weeks, Meyer.

MEYER
>Goodbye, Benny.

BUGSY smiles his radiant, ferocious smile for the last time, doffs his hat, and disappears down the hallway, leaving MEYER alone in the shadows.

CUT TO

EXT. AIRPORT - NIGHT

BUGSY is hurrying towards his plane, holding his hat on his head and clutching his coat under his arm.

CUT TO

INT. OFFICE - NIGHT

MEYER is leaving for the night. He puts on his hat and takes his briefcase, waving goodbye to his employees.

CUT TO

INT. AIRPLANE - NIGHT

BUGSY is reading a newspaper. A stewardess is serving drinks to the other passengers. After a moment, BUGSY looks pensively out the window at the country passing by underneath him.

CUT TO

INT. CAR - NIGHT

MEYER is being driven home, his briefcase on the seat beside him. Like BUGSY, he is looking out the window, seemingly entranced by the lights as they pass by, glinting in the raindrops.

CUT TO

EXT. AIRPORT - NIGHT

BUGSY is disembarking from the plane. The stewardesses smile as the passengers descend the gangplank.

CUT TO

EXT. MEYER'S APARTMENT BUILDING - NIGHT

MEYER gets out of the car, waves to the driver and goes up the steps. The doorman tips his hat to him as he opens the doors.

CUT TO

EXT. AIRPORT - NIGHT

BUGSY walks out of the terminal and sees his driver waiting for him. The driver tips his cap and BUGSY gets in the back seat. The car pulls away under the moonless sky.

CUT TO

INT. MEYER'S APARTMENT - NIGHT

MEYER unlocks the door and comes in. His steps echo in the large, empty rooms. He puts his coat over a chair and pours himself a drink.

CUT TO

EXT. VIRGINIA HILL'S HOME - NIGHT

BUGSY's car pulls up in front of VIRGINIA's house. He gets out, waves to the driver, and goes inside.

CUT TO

INT. MEYER'S APARTMENT - NIGHT

MEYER sits down in a chair in the hallway, next to a small table with a lamp and a telephone phone. He is disheveled, his tie loosened, his shirt unbuttoned. He sips his drink, then puts it on the table.

He sits there. Silent, motionless, waiting.

                                                                    CUT TO

INT. VIRGINIA HILL'S HOME - NIGHT

BUGSY closes the door behind him, throws his briefcase on a chair and goes into the living room.

BUGSY
        Ginny! You home?

There is no answer. He goes to the liquor cabinet and pours himself a drink. He takes off his jacket and throws it on top of his briefcase, unbuttons his shirt and loosens his tie. Picking up his newspaper, he relaxes into an easy chair and puts his feet up.

We HOLD on him for a long moment as he reads and sips his drink.

Then, SLOWLY, we PAN LEFT over to the window. We RACK FOCUS until we can faintly see a black car parked across the street, nearly hidden in the shadows.

Almost soundlessly, three bulletholes CRACK one by one through the window, leaving white fractures snaking across the glass. We RACK FOCUS again, so we see only these shattered cracks in the glass, as we hear, far off, A CAR'S ENGINE START AND DRIVE AWAY.

Slowly, we PAN RIGHT until we return to BUGSY, but now all we see is a bloodstained hand still gripping his newspaper.

A phone RINGS. Shrill and piercing. One, two, three, four times. On the fifth ring, we...

                                                                    CUT TO

INT. MEYER'S APARTMENT - NIGHT

The phone next to MEYER is ringing. He seems not to react, staring off into space. Finally, ON THE TENTH RING, he picks up the phone.

MEYER
        Yeah?

He listens. We cannot hear what is being said on the other end of the line.

MEYER
        When?

Pause.

MEYER
    Ok.

He hangs up the phone. He seems to shrink down into his chair. He runs his hands through his hair wearily and then rubs his eyes.

CLOSE UP of MEYER. His face is crumbling. Tears begin to well up in his eyes.

                                                    MATCH CUT TO

EXT. JERUSALEM CAFE - DAY

CLOSE UP of the OLD MEYER. His eyes are hidden by sunglasses, but his head is cocked at the same, sunken angle. He looks up suddenly, and stares directly into the CAMERA.

MEYER
    I know what you think.

REVERSE SHOT of YOSSI KLEIN, his face a mask of shock and pity.

MEYER
    You think I didn't love him, like my own brother. You think I didn't weep when they
    told me...

He stops, his voice chokes.

MEYER
    You pity me. You despise me. Well who the fuck are you? Who the fuck are you?! He
    was a crazy kid. I did everything I could for him. Everything... Do you pity me? Do you?

YOSSI looks down at his coffee.

MEYER
    You don't understand. You're young, you don't understand. What you make for them...
    In the end... they take it back. (Pause.) Get out of here. (Another pause.) Get out of here!

YOSSI nods, puts some money on the table and gets up to go. For a moment, he turns back.

YOSSI
    I do pity you. I'm sorry.

CLOSE UP of MEYER'S FACE. The face of a broken old man. His head is bent as if by the tremendous weight of his past. Behind his impenetrable sunglasses, there are tears in his eyes.

                                                    CUT TO BLACK

THE FOLLOWING TITLES APPEAR:

MEYER LANSKY WAS DENIED ISRAELI CITIZENSHIP UNDER THE LAW OF RETURN. HE RETURNED TO THE UNITED STATES, WHERE HE DIED IN FLORIDA IN 1980. HE WAS NEVER CONVICTED OF A SINGLE CRIME.

BUGSY SIEGEL'S KILLERS WERE NEVER FOUND. HIS MURDER REMAINS UNSOLVED

THE END

www.ingramcontent.com/pod-product-compliance
Lightning Source LLC
Chambersburg PA
CBHW081259170526
45165CB00011B/3350